The
90-Second
Therapist

The
90-Second
Therapist

Timothy Bentley M.Div.

Summerhill Press
Toronto

© 1988 Timothy Bentley

Published by:
Summerhill Press Ltd.
Toronto, Ontario

Printed and bound in Canada

Canadian Cataloguing in Publication Data

Bentley, Timothy, 1943-
   The 90-second therapist

ISBN 0-920197-44-2

1. Psychology, Applied. 2. Self-help techniques.
I. Title.

BF636. B45 1988   158'.1   C88-093616-9

Dedication

The 90-Second Therapist is dedicated to the co-founder of the Toronto Centre For The Family, an excellent therapist, and my wife, Esther Leah Kohn-Bentley. Esther is an extraordinary human being, the brightest, warmest, and most loving person I have ever known. One of her finest qualities, which has deeply influenced both my personal life and my style as a therapist, is her commitment to living life to the fullest. That idea runs from one end of this book to the other.

Because Esther and I have for years shared every aspect of our work, have supervised each other, seen clients together, designed and taught courses jointly, and in our personal life have loved, fought, and raised children together, her ideas flow through this book as much as do my own. I would be at a loss to distinguish her contribution to *The 90-Second Therapist* from mine.

Finally, despite her own busy practice, Esther has found the energy to shelter me when I needed time and quiet to write, to challenge me, to uphold me when weary, and to edit my every careless word ruthlessly.

Words can only hint at how highly I think of her.

Timothy Bentley
The Toronto Centre for the Family

Foreword

We live in the most emotionally complicated age this world has ever seen. As the twentieth century rolls toward the twenty-first, the number of possibilities, and potential problems, in our relationships is approaching infinity.

In the material world, almost everything we desire is now within reach; the only limitation is a technology whose capabilities are still multiplying geometrically. But in our inner world and our relationships, things look very different. Here our limitations are all too obvious.

True, our natural desire for perfection is constantly being whetted. Popular films and novels transport us into the world of the strong, the true, the hilarious, and the erotic. We are easy targets for the mass marketing of desire. Advertising tempts us with air-brushed models carefully arranged in their flawless studio homes.

But the rest of us, real people with dust on our shelves, sleep in our eyes, thinning hair, softening tummies, and short legs, have to work with innate emotional equipment not much improved over that of our cave-dwelling ancestors. Our ability to handle anger and sadness, fear and joy, and a host of other feelings is limited, yet the complexity of our lives brings on wave after wave of emotions which buffet us and sometimes threaten to drown us completely.

While we long to live out some of the best of the media images, our primitive feelings often thwart those hopes. And the uncontrolled tides of our emotions keep shaking us up, although we wish for inner peace and satisfying loves....Good relationships bring us moments of surprising joy. They challenge our self-defeating narcissism, and they uphold us when we are in pain. But today we ask more of our family, friends, and lovers than the human race has ever required them to deliver. In addition, as a society, we have blundered into a social-emotional situation within which, ironically, relationships are more difficult to maintain than they have ever been.

In that context, I hope that busy people will benefit from a book like this, a collection of short, sensible, bite-size thoughts, tested ideas that can make a difference to how you approach this challenging time. Many of the ideas presented here started out as part of a 90-second radio "column", broadcast nationally each weekday. Because radio demands both brevity and relevance, it challenged me to condense my experience with clients and my reading of therapeutic literature into a compact and accessible form.

The 90-Second Therapist is designed to help you understand yourself, get the most out of your relationships, and give your best too.

Thoughtful cynics, who know that my usual style is to spend patient weeks and months in therapy with my clients, have sometimes asked, "How much can you really say in 90 seconds?" To which I have been known flippantly to reply, "It depends how fast I talk."

But the truth is that, no matter how quickly or slowly I talk, people tell me that they have found this format remarkably effective, seeing these ideas as provocative beginnings to their own thought processes, rather than as complete tracts about mine. They phone me or stop me to say things like, "Send me a copy of what you said. I need to read it and think more about it." Or, "I make a point of listening to you every day, because what you say always makes sense." Or, "You're the one person on the air who always seems to understand what I'm dealing with." While flattered by these comments, I also recognize that the beauty these ideas possess originates in the eye of the beholder, whenever readers or listeners see them as reflections of their own lives.

So here they are, in print. The best way to use *The 90-Second Therapist* may be the way you drink a glass of orange juice or take a vitamin at breakfast. In other words, let it serve as a quick daily challenge or inspiration. Give yourself the gift of 90 seconds to read just one selection, and then try putting its ideas into action throughout the day.

Use these pages as a spur to your own thoughts.

Trust your instincts.

Run with your dreams.

Let yourself become the 90-Second Therapist.

Acknowledgements

I am grateful to the following people who have contributed, directly and indirectly, to the creation of this book:

My wife Esther, to whom it is dedicated. My son Erin, who, at the age of eleven, did much of the preliminary editing to convert broadcast scripts into the pages of a book. His facility with computers and word-processing made my task easier, and his interest in my ideas greatly encouraged me. My stepchildren, Trisha and Andrew, who have taught me much of what I know about the blended family, the role of the stepfather, and the exciting development of teenagers. They, with Esther and Erin, have provided me a loving atmosphere in which to carry out this work.

My parents, Alice and Michael Bentley, who encouraged me in both broadcasting and writing from the early age of thirteen.

Marilyn Laiken and Jeff Solway, caring friends whose profound understanding of organizations has frequently inspired me.

Specialists in various fields who have offered me their friendship and professional support: Dr. John Axler, Dr. Mario Bartoletti, the Rev. Tim Elliot, the Rev. Tim Foley, Jim Ford, John Goodwin, Frances Harwood, the Rev. Betty Kilbourn, the Rev. Tom Kingston, Dr. Barbara Landau, Dr. Ellen Levine, Prof. Steve Levine, the Rev. John Oldham, Prof. Berel Schiff, Fred Schloessinger, Kathleen Keating-Schloessinger, Christine Sutherland.

At the CKO radio network, where this book had its origins: Jim Connell, Colleen MacDonell, Al Michaels, Melanie Reffes, Rob Whitehead. At the Canadian Broadcasting Corporation, where my love of media flourished: Roy Bonisteel, Harry Brown, Brian Freeland, Hana Gartner, Sig Gerber, Doug MacDonald,

Knowlton Nash, Leo Rampen.

I also owe endless thanks to a superb research staff: my clients. By sharing their life experiences with me, they have inspired me to write these pages and reinforced my convictions about self-therapy. For the sake of privacy, I have disguised both their identities and their names. If you think that you recognize someone I have mentioned, you can be quite sure that you are wrong, for I have deliberately given out misleading clues and at times combined their stories.

Finally, I acknowledge the late Donald Winnicott M.D., F.R.C.P., Britain's pioneer in children's psychiatry, and also my godfather, whose books first taught me about the way parents function as therapists to their children. An example of special interest to me is a passage from his book *The Child, the Family and the Outside World*, in which he describes the actual first few days of my life, in London during the Second World War:

> I know a young mother who made a very early contact with her baby boy, her first child. From the day of his birth, after each feed, he was put in a cradle and left by his mother's bed by the sensible matron of the nursing home. For a while he would lie awake in the quiet of the room, and the mother would put down her hand to him; and before he was a week old he began to catch hold of her fingers and look up in her direction. This intimate relationship continued without interruption and developed, and I believe it has helped to lay the foundation for the child's personality and for what we call his emotional development, and his capacity to withstand the frustrations and shocks that sooner or later came his way.

I will always be grateful to Winnicott for this brief perspective on my young life. It reminds me that, from the beginning, my own therapist was there for me, reaching out to help heal the fear induced by the bombing each night, buttressing the foundations of my personality.

Writing Th*e 90-Second Therapist* I have also been inspired by the fact that Winnicott's early books also originated as broadcasts, on BBC radio during the 1940s. I enjoy a delightful sense of treading, unknown to him, in his footsteps.

Table of Contents

Who is the 90-Second Therapist?

Who is the 90-Second Therapist?

The question is intriguing, because in an obvious sense the 90-Second Therapist is me, as I read my daily minute-and-a-half script on the air. And yet....

The word "psycho-therapist" comes from Greek words meaning "to heal the soul." We generally think about therapists as a group of specially trained and experienced professionals who work in offices, growth centres, hospitals, and mental health agencies. They practise according to the dictates of a particular school of therapy and see their patients by appointment only. Of course, that is an entirely valid way of looking at the word "therapist." And later in these pages, I will talk some more about this way of doing therapy.

At times, we broaden the meaning of "therapist" to include nurses or doctors, or lawyers or religious leaders, when they are operating at their most empathic level. Some people even get relief from their emotional pressures by letting down their hair when they talk with their hairdressers. But the problem, you see, is that we are still restricting the use of the term to professional life.

Let's look at this notion of the "healing of the soul" from another perspective.

Seen in this new light, since the dawn of time, billions of therapists have walked this earth. I am not restricting this title to shamans, medicine men and women, priests or witch doctors, although they have all certainly functioned as therapists. No, in this light, there are and always have been therapists—or healers—in most homes around the world. In this sense, at their best, parents are therapists to their children, not only concerned with their physical well-being, but encouraging them to talk about what they feel, teaching them how to get along with others, and helping them resolve emotional conflicts caused by fear and dependency and self-centredness.

In this sense, married people at their best are therapists to their relationships, probing together to maintain the health of their partnership and to understand the unseen currents which might otherwise sweep them out of love and out of joy.

In this sense, at their best, true friends are therapists to each other, saying "You can tell me anything and everything. I will not betray you. And by talking your problems out, you will gain new insights and discover happier ways of living."

Finally, at our best, we are therapists or healers to our selves every time we entertain thoughts such as, "I'm acting strangely today. I'm not my best self. I should pay attention to what's going on in my feelings."

So, in our private lives, we are therapists every day. We may not have the benefit of the quiet office, the closed door, and the 50-minute hour. We may have to snatch a minute of conversation here, 30 seconds of reflection there, for these most urgent and priceless of all human encounters. These moments spent healing ourselves are beyond price—without them, this would be a grey and sick old world, and all of us but shadows of our full potential.

Who is the 90-Second Therapist? Professionals are always tempted, as we jealously guard our territory against the encroachment of the unscrupulous, to reserve the term "therapist" for ourselves. It is certainly a temptation to answer that the 90-Second Therapist is Timothy Bentley.

But honesty whispers that "Day by day, hour by hour, it is you." True enough, in my professional capacity, I may provide the context and the expertise to nurture and advance the healing, but I am not the healer. And that is very good news, because it locates the power of healing exactly where it belongs.

No, it is not me.

The 90-Second Therapist is you.

Nothing in this book is intended to suggest that people suffering emotional distress should avoid professional psychotherapy. On the contrary, anyone who is experiencing serious discomfort, in particular, severe anxiety, severe depression, or suicidal or violent thoughts, whether on a purely personal level or in the context of particular relationships, is hereby advised to seek professional help from the most competent practitioners, at once.

CHAPTER ONE

Understanding Myself

"Know thyself," the sages of ancient Greece commanded their hearers. Their advanced civilization recognized that self-understanding is the foundation for all human friendship. Twenty-five hundred years later, that has not changed.

Without a working knowledge of our spirits, our mysterious inner ways, it is impossible either to enjoy, or to give pleasure to, those we most care about; it is the self that supports, and sometimes sabotages, our relationships.

Without an open-hearted love for ourselves, we cannot hope to love others.

A SKETCH OF SELF-ESTEEM

Do you like yourself?

Do you see the cup as half-full or half-empty?

Do you expect that people will treat you with respect?

Your answers to those three questions reveal a lot about your self-esteem.

Here's a quick sketch of what self-esteem looks like. People with high self-esteem tend to be appealing, and fairly confident. They enjoy their own company and get along well with others.

Those with low self-esteem are seldom attractive, except to bullies and users. They lack self-confidence, even if they have achieved success in their careers. They don't like themselves much, and they often carry around a load of unresolved anger toward others.

Where do you fit into that scheme?

If your self-esteem is not as high as you want it to be, you can do something about it, though I can promise no quick or easy answers. This task will require time, commitment, and a willing sense of adventure.

You see, as children, we all experienced failures. If these were emphasized at home, at play, and at school, without being balanced by praise, we gradually developed a mechanism in our mind like a tape recorder constantly repeating "I am not worthy."

To some extent everyone, even in adulthood, suffers from that repeated message. But when for certain people, the volume on that recording is constantly turned up high, their self-esteem remains chronically low.

Fortunately, there are some things you can do on your own to turn down the volume. Such as not taking your faults so seriously. And when someone pays you a compliment, being certain to hear it, to take it in.

You can make a list on paper of your good qualities or ask someone you trust what he or she thinks about you.

Whatever you decide to do, it will be well worth the trouble, because in the process you are bound to discover some delightful, half-forgotten, aspects of your fine personality.

And as your self-esteem rises, so will your enjoyment of life itself.

LEARNING TO COPE WITH STRESS

As our society's stress level rises out of sight, drugs and alcohol are controlling the lives of some of our brightest lights. High-profile personalities such as Mary Tyler Moore, Chevy Chase, and Elizabeth Taylor have publicly admitted that they were once hooked. But are there better answers to today's high stress levels? I think so.

The use of alcohol, marijuana, and cocaine has become a crisis for two major reasons. The first is that there is a lot of money floating around our society, and that is not likely to change.

The other reason is that most people feel over-stressed, and under-relaxed, and, for some, it seems an easy solution to swig, puff, snort, sniff, or pump a chemical into their system. A Hollywood counsellor has estimated that one-third of the addicted movie and TV people in his city got that way from "trying to relax."

So, if you're feeling the stress of life, here are three safe alternatives to drugs and alcohol that will help you.

1. Check out your priorities. Is the search for success leading you down the garden path? Is the quest for money twisting your stomach into knots?

2. Make use of natural tranquillizers like going for a walk, getting a massage, or playing with a child.

3. Work on your relationships. There's nothing like a warm supportive friendship or marriage to soothe you when you're jangled.

People who deal well with stress also tend to raise the morale of those around them, and to be more productive at home and at work.

So calm down, naturally. You owe it to yourself—and your loved ones.

EMOTIONS AND THE SELF THERAPIST

In order to be a 90-Second Therapist, you need to be able to feel and express your emotions. I devote a great deal of attention in therapy to helping my clients tune in to their feelings, so that when they are finished working with me they have a whole new attitude to their emotions, one where they are deeply curious about them and take them seriously as part of their daily life.

One path to becoming your own therapist is to challenge yourself with questions about your emotions such as those I would ask if you were seated comfortably in my office:

What are your feeling right now? Is that emotion changing as you think about it? Does it remind you of an old feeling that you have had? Did you ever feel like this as a child?

Do you trust this feeling? Could it be bringing you important information about how you function as a human being? Does it drive you to behave in ways that you wouldn't deliberately choose?

If your feelings are unhappy or uncomfortable, how do you usually deal with them: shove them into a closet, or let yourself experience them? And what usually happens then? And do you allow yourself to savour the happy, serene, or passionate feelings that come your way? Again, what happens then?

As a therapist, I have an unrelenting interest in my own and other people's emotions, because they function like the engine of the human spirit, propelling us into misery when we ignore them, and into happiness as we accept and harness them.

THERE'S MORE TO CRISES THAN DANGER

There is said to be a single Chinese word for "crisis" which conveys its meaning very cleverly through two quite separate and very different thoughts: danger and opportunity.

Both danger and opportunity were clearly evident in the situation of a young man named Peter, who came to visit me in the midst of a serious life crisis.

A few days before, to his complete surprise, his wife had walked out on him and said she would never return. Peter was understandably in a state of total shock.

In his situation, the idea that there is danger involved in crisis needs no further explanation. It was all too obvious that Peter was desperately hurt and in danger of suffering even more. But what Peter never expected was that this crisis in his life would also provide him with a special opportunity for growth.

Because Peter was so desperate for support and insight into his situation, we began recording his session on videotape and letting him play them back at home on his VCR.

Peter was fascinated by what he learned as he watched the screen. There he saw, in living colour, things he had never known about himself.

He noticed how he avoided dealing with topics that felt threatening to him, by changing the subject. And how he covered up his discomfort in relationships with laughter.

In other words, he saw on videotape how, unwittingly, he had contributed to the destruction of his marriage.

If you were in a crisis today, you might have the same sense of danger, and you might turn it into a similar opportunity.

But why wait for the videotape?

You could achieve the same thing by taking time to play back the tapes of your life in your imagination, and watch yourself repeat whatever destructive patterns may have endangered your happiness down through the years.

You could then take that opportunity to grow and to change, to ensure that you don't drift through your life playing the same unhappy old roles.

But, on second thought, why wait for a crisis? You don't really need danger to seize an opportunity.

DREAMS: A LOOK INTO OUR INNER DEPTHS

It took a very frightening nightmare to help Martin change the course of his career for the better. But for the dream to help him, he had to pay attention to it.

On the surface, Martin appeared to be the happy and very successful chairman of a major financial firm. But one dark night, he had a terrible dream. He was on a ship that was sinking in the middle of the ocean. In the dream, he jumped into a lifeboat and rowed and rowed, until he reached a large, safe mountain, which he then went on to climb.

Martin's dream helped this very rational man listen to the nonrational part of his unconscious mind. He came to realize how much he really wanted to abandon ship—which meant leaving a career which was beginning to falter—and to embark on his own private business. The tall mountain symbolized the challenge he was facing.

We call it the *unconscious* for good reason. Although by far the largest part of the mind, it operates silently, under the surface of consciousness. Deep below our awareness, it constantly processes vast amounts of data—dreams, memories, emotions.

And while we can never know all its contents with our conscious minds, when we pay attention to our dreams, we can depend on receiving life-changing insights.

DREAMS: LEARNING TO READ THEIR MEANING

Jamie had never thought much about his dreams, but this one really caught his attention. A tornado was tearing a path of destruction though the homes in his neighbourhood. Throughout this wild and devastating storm, Jamie's house, a good, solid brick structure, remained firm and undamaged.

Thinking about it afterward, Jamie was excited about the dream, and not only because of its dramatic elements. He had a hunch it meant something very important.

He realized that for months he had felt himself to be in danger in the midst of an emotional storm. Job problems, family stress, and a nagging sense of self-doubt were all taking their toll on his peace of mind.

The function of this particular dream at this particular time was to help him discover that he was much more solid and secure in his "house," the dream's symbol for his personality, than ever before.

This important and reassuring information led him to take more initiative in his work and family relationships. As they improved, he began, to feel even better about himself, discovering that he had much more to give than he had ever recognized.

Like Jamie, many people wonder what our dreams are for and how they work. No one understands dreams completely: there are as many kinds of dreams as there are people. But there is no question that all of us dream, whether or not we remember doing so. In fact most people dream several times a night, for a total of approximately two hours.

Dreams are a means of sorting out and re-balancing our feelings about our lives. Their function is a hygienic one, the emotional equivalent of brushing our teeth; if we fail to dream for long enough, we will probably suffer the intolerable agony of pent-up emotion.

On the brighter side, one delightful side-effect of our dreams is that, like people in all ages and on every continent, we can learn more about ourselves through paying attention to them. As Jamie discovered, they can offer an encouraging update on our progress in the secret centre of our lives.

If you are becoming curious about the meaning of your dreams, here are three things you can do which will help you make sense of them.

First, help yourself remember them by writing them down. Many people keep a pencil and paper beside their bed, and write down a few words about their dreams as soon as they awake.

Those who record their dreams have discovered an interesting secondary result, that making an effort to remember their dreams seems to reassure the unconscious mind that they are interested in what it has to say. Then they find themselves remembering and understanding their dreams more spontaneously.

Next, give yourself a few moments of quiet to think about your dreams. Dreams have an evanescent quality, and they are unlikely to intrude into your thought if you are always distracted by other interests.

Then, look for the larger patterns in your dreams, before you try to understand the minute details. For instance, a child often dreamt of cycling around and around a tiny planet where he never met anyone else. To understand this dream, don't bother trying to figure out the symbolism of the bicycle or the round planet, which in another dream might have considerable significance.

Look instead at the extreme loneliness of the child which pervades the dreams, not only isolated in outer space but also totally alone on this small planet. Clearly this dream is a cry for help from the unconscious. "Find me, save me, hold me," the dream calls out. "Help me connect."

Such a dream, often repeated, and containing repetitious actions, can tell you that your mind is struggling to cope with some constantly troubling aspect of your life.

Finally, as you begin to interpret your dreams, do it with a light, even a metaphorical, touch. For instance, it you often dream about warfare, it doesn't necessarily mean that you are a violent person who wishes to kill people. It could indicate that you feel yourself embattled, in constant danger, surrounded by emotionally dangerous situations. The dream provides a good warning: it is time to get some support, find allies, deal with situations in your life that endanger your well-being.

Dreams may even play on words. For instance, in the film *Still of the Night*, the plot turned on a dream about a green box, which actually stood for a character called "Greenbacks." In another context, a word like "fodder" might actually refer to "father."

Sometimes people will say to a friend or therapist, "Here's my dream. Interpret it," assuming that there are such things as standard interpretations. Better to gaze at your remembered dreams as you would a beautiful painting. The more you admire it, the more you cherish it, the more its meaning will gradually reveal itself.

Equipped with better information about your inner self derived from your dreams, you will find yourself like Jamie, more self confident and more effective in the world of your outer self and relationships.

LEARNING FROM MEMBERS OF YOUR OWN SEX

A lot of today's sensitive men developed their sensitivity by studying the women in their lives. They learned from women how to feel their own emotions, how to keep a relationship alive and healthy, and how to be gentle.

In many ways the process itself has been wonderfully humanizing, but the way it happened sometimes left behind a trail of destruction.

Some of these men began by studying their wives, and when they had learned all that their wives had to teach them, they took lovers and studied in their boudoirs.

In the process, of course, they damaged their primary relationships and in many cases became, at best, only pale imitations of their flesh-and-blood women, because they learned to feel, but not to value their own male strength.

Ironically, like reflections caught in trick mirrors, women were also learning from men. And, in their own ways, exposing themselves to danger.

Some, for instance, lacking powerful females to model themselves on, became assertive just like the male stereotype—tough, isolated, chronically angry. And they allied themselves with certain so-called masculine values, in particular the idea of success in business at any price.

Since then, they have been paying the same price as men, in damage to their family life and to their health. As a result of all this social upheaval and experimentation with roles, one not-very-surprising fact has become clear: that the very best models for women today are women, and for men, men.

The good news is that in most parts of the country, men's groups and women's groups have developed, where self-therapists can stretch the wings of their personalities.

In that open and sharing atmosphere, they can grow in their understanding that only members of their own sex can offer.

CHANGE: FEAR AND DESIRE

How many therapists does it take to change a light bulb? You've probably heard this one before. The usual answer is five. One to hold the bulb and four to turn the ladder.

But in fact it takes only one therapist to change a light bulb. There is, of course, one condition: the light bulb has to really want to change.

It's a clever joke because it pokes fun at an essential truth about life. Good therapy requires much more that a good therapist. In fact, therapists are utterly helpless unless, deep down, their clients want to change.

Change is essential to therapy simply because it is essential to life. From the moment we are born until the day we die, we live in the midst of change. The seasons and the landscape, our relationships and our society, in short all facets of our environment, are constantly shifting.

When we respond to a changing world with inner transformations that suit both our character and the shifting circumstances around us, then life tends to be good, and our minds remain healthy.

When, on the other hand, we refuse to grow, and remain stuck in the ruts we travelled in five years ago, or even last week, life can be very depressing and very bleak.

So most healthy people have a basic desire for change.

Yet, paradoxically, most also fear it, for to change means to enter the unknown. And because that can be pretty scary, even sensible people sometimes wish they could just keep everything the same.

This is where a good friend, a committed lover, or a caring family member can function as a 90-Second Therapist for you. Just by listening with warmth and concern, such a person can provide that much-needed feeling of security which encourages human transformation.

OUR MOODS AFFECT OUR HEALTH

Do you know that you can fight disease by the way you think?

In the 1970s, two doctors, Carl and Stephanie Simonton, were branded as "quacks" when they claimed that cancer patients whom they treated with counselling, including guided images of themselves as healthy people, were more likely to survive than those who had only conventional treatment, that is, radiation and chemotherapy.

Conventional medicine has generally pictured the body's defence system as an army that operates independently of the control of the brain. According to this model, our thoughts, fantasies, and emotions have no connection at all with how we cope with illness. But now a new science is challenging this view and interesting the medical establishment. This science is called psycho-neuro immunology and suggests that the Simontons may have been right all along, that our brains can help, or hinder, our physical defence systems.

So what does all this mean to non-medical people like you and me? It suggests that our moods may affect our health. That if we suffer from depression, or anxiety, or hopelessness for a long time, we may become more susceptible to diseases—from the common cold to cancer—and less likely to recover quickly.

It means that becoming your own 90-Second Therapist is no frill, when tough situations in your work life and relationships have locked you into chronic emotional pain.

It tells you, in fact, that the old "ignore it and maybe it will go away" routine may constitute a gamble with your health.

OUR FOODS AFFECT OUR MOODS

There is a well-known old saying that "You are what you eat." It's true, but not just in terms of muscle tissue. Your foods affect your moods.

When people describe themselves as "sleepless," or "racing," or "tense and depressed," there are usually verifiable upsetting events in their lives which are responsible for some of the symptoms.

But ask how much coffee, tea or chocolate they take in, and you will frequently discover that they themselves have been making their tension worse, by taking in too much caffeine.

You don't have to be under terrible stress to discover that a huge chocolate chip cookie before bedtime can leave your sleep shallow and unsatisfying. Just ask me about it.

Or look at another mood-altering substance: Sugar. Plenty of already-depressed people feel even worse because they take in too much sugar. Their bodies become so preoccupied with dumping out the excess that they don't leave enough behind to keep their energy up. People who eat a lot of sugar usually feel tired and cranky much of the time.

And those who don't eat enough food for breakfast and lunch often feel much the same, even more so if whatever they do eat is sweet, like a bowl of coco puffs or a quick candy bar and coffee.

Another dangerous food is alcohol. People who are depressed and tired often reach for a drink. They tell themselves it will "pick them up," but the truth is that alcohol is a depressant to an already-unhappy psyche, they have actually written themselves a recipe for more despair.

On top of these obvious, universal situations, it is also possible that you may have an individual allergic reaction to other substances which shows itself emotionally.

Many people are unaware of the emotional influence of wheat flour, milk, and chemical additives, to name just a few. If you think you may be sensitive, it is certainly worth getting tested.

You could waste a lot of energy trying to prop yourself up emotionally, when just eating the right foods can help bring on bright moods.

GOOD HEALTH: LUCK OR CHOICE?

Many of us tend to think about good health or illness as a matter of heredity, or luck. But today, increasingly, we have to recognize that physical health is a matter of personal choice.

There is no question that some people are born with a tendency to disease and that others lose their health unavoidably through accidents. But as the cost of health care rises, governments and insurers have begun to face the fact that many of today's expensive illnesses are caused by people's own deliberate choices.

Look at the high-stress jobs people choose: air traffic controllers, policemen, broadcasters, etc. Like players of Russian Roulette, they know there is always a chance that the pressure will lead to an ulcer, a heart attack, or a stroke. If they're lucky, they escape with "only" asthma, eczema, or hives.

Or consider lifestyle. Most people get less exercise than a hibernating groundhog, and at the same time many risk their health by eating too much food with too few nutrients, drinking too much alcohol, and smoking cigarettes.

Finally, many people live with the stress of unhealthy relationships. Relationships that are chronically painful, whether with parents or children, lovers or spouses, can lead to physical illness and take years off our lives.

What's the answer? We return to the idea of choice.

Rather than waiting for trouble to ambush them, sensible people everywhere are taking their health care into their own hands. They are recognizing that as they choose a healthier lifestyle—in terms of environment, exercise, relationships, and food, alcohol and tobacco intake—they are increasing the likelihood of being physically comfortable.

One of the intangible rewards of their improvement in physical health is a greater feeling of emotional happiness.

HOW SINGLES KEEP THEMSELVES THAT WAY

If you are in your mid-thirties, single and wish you were not, by now you will have wondered, "Is it just bad luck, have I met the wrong kind of people, or could the major reason I am single be me?"

There are two common ways that people who would rather be in pairs manage to keep themselves single.

The first is: they deny that they are attractive. Probably, when they were children, their parents were too messed up, or stressed out, to really let the love flow. As kids, maybe they were the recipients of anger and criticism much of the time.

However it happened, many single people did not develop that strong inner core that asserts, "I'm worthy, I'm attractive." As a form of self-protection, they have learned to keep themselves separate from others much of the time, some passively by hiding in the corners, others actively by being rude and aggressive.

The second factor that keeps some people single is that they have never learned how to give or understood the importance of giving. These are people whom others tend to avoid, because most people can smell a "taker" from a mile away.

Takers are those who are mainly interested in getting their own needs met at the expense of others, whether that means getting fed, getting laid, getting babies, or getting supported financially. It is not an attractive style.

The bad news is that these two factors, low self-esteem and taking, are often linked. If you don't know how to love yourself, how can you ever expect to be generous to others?

The good news is that low self-esteem is not a terminal condition. Whether in their mid-thirties or mid-seventies, anyone can grow in self-esteem.

As they like themselves more, people who may once have been takers will have less need to use other people. They will find that their healthy love for themselves naturally spreads to those special persons in their lives as well.

So while they may end up getting fed, laid, pregnant, and rich, they also give as much as they get. And they will learn to love that experience of giving.

WAYS FOR SINGLES TO MAKE NEW FRIENDS

If you are a single person frustrated with the difficulty of meeting other singles, know that you are not alone. Many people talk with me about how to meet people, to find a friend who may ultimately become a lover.

Now that the church social has gone the way of the horse and buggy, these people say there are not a lot of good places to meet other singles. For certain, the "meat markets" of the bar scene, are a definite loser. Few people come home from that noisy, smoky, competitive atmosphere with solid relationships.

They are much more likely to bring home a one-night stand, a headache, or a social disease.

One of the best ways to make friends is to get involved in a group of new people where sex and dating are not the main focus.

Taking a course is an obvious example, especially if you choose topics which are likely to attract people of the opposite sex.

For instance, a woman who wants to meet men might study auto mechanics, since there are bound to be quite a few men in the class. And it is a very practical topic for women to study, even if only to avoid being taken for a ride at the garage. Another option is photography. While you're focussing on lenses and developing your art, you'll also be interacting with men who have similar interests. So there is a good chance that two of you might just click—or flash.

The same approach works for men. You're bound to meet more women in a gourmet cooking or dance exercise course than at a wrestling class. This may sound like the plot for a situation comedy, but it actually works.

Another proven way to meet compatible people is working for a good cause. As part of a political party or a volunteer organization, you can accomplish something you believe in and, at the same time, become part of a lively social entity.

By meeting other people with values similar to yours, you may soon find yourself enjoying a full-blooded relationship with someone who appeals to your mind without giving you a headache.

PREPARING FOR A HAPPY RETIREMENT

Around the age of 55 or 60, people often start to get anxious. Anxious about retirement, that is.

At that age, beginning to contemplate letting go of the security of the work world, you and your relative or friend can make preparations which will lead to greater happiness and emotional well-being in retirement.

A broadcasting executive in his early sixties was talking about that recently. "I'd like to cut back soon to working three days a week," he said. "I want to make the transition gradual."

His sensible awareness is in startling contrast to the many people who fail to prepare themselves for retirement at all. Their comfortable illusion is that if you ignore the issue, it will take care of itself eventually.

Usually they find the event utterly traumatic. We have all watched as some, men especially fall apart emotionally after they stop working, and sometimes lose even their health in the process.

It happens because they have made their work their entire life.

Unless they have invested as heavily in their marriages and other relationships over the years as they have in their jobs, they may find that they have very little to offer there, once they are at home 24 hours a day.

More that one wife has confided in fearful anticipation, "I get scared, thinking about old Frank's retirement. I can't imagine having him under my feet all the time."

So be good to yourself and your loved ones. Here are three ways to prepare yourself for retirement:

First, if you have not paid enough attention to your marriage or friendships, now is the time to start talking and start listening. Your "people" skills will make or break your retirement.

Second, make sure you have hobbies, sports, and other interests to keep you stimulated during those unfamiliar days when you don't have a job to go to.

Third, like the broadcaster, talk with your boss about tapering off rather than quitting cold turkey. It may take some convincing, but it's certainly worth trying. It doesn't pay to be the all-or-nothing type when you are thinking about retirement.

YOUR SEARCH FOR MEANING

Helen, a minister, once told me she was afraid that therapy was making her self-centred. "All this concern about my feelings and my relationships!" she exclaimed. "Is that all there is to life?"

As a sensitive person raised to always "think of others first," Helen was keenly aware that those who gaze only at their navels may lose sight of the needs of those around them and forget their responsibility to make the world a better place.

In other words, she was questioning the spiritual implications of therapy.

I replied that in my experience those who have learned how to act as their own therapists actually have much more to give, both to those who are close to them and to the larger world. In fact, the process of becoming your own therapist is a spiritual quest.

What are we trying to express when we use the word "spirituality?"

Each person tries to describe it in a different way, some using religious formulas, others their own personal terms. But no one seems to find spirituality easy to define, because it relies on no creeds, rules, dogmas, or orthodoxy, and boasts no Rome, no Canterbury, no Mecca, and no Salt Lake City.

Its capitals can only be found in the human heart, and its authority derives only from the individual's inner experience.

But many people have agreed on this much about the nature of spirituality: it has a searching quality, seeking to discover the meaning of the individual's life along with a satisfying way to relate to the world around.

THE MEANING OF ME

Without even knowing it, you may be asking yourself profound spiritual questions. Sometimes in calm, sometimes in crisis, you are probably grappling with the meaning of your own life.

Your private questions ae echoed in a growing public curiosity about the implications of spirituality. Examples include the enthusiasic response to such widely differing phenomena as the love ethic of Leo Buscalia and the reincarnation experiences of Shirley Maclaine.

But ultimately you will find that you can rely on no celebrity and no therapist to provide the answers. In fact, as you become your own therapist, you will take possession of your own spirituality, searching within and without for the significance of your life.

Rather than waiting until personal crises like the approach of death force the question, "Am I only dust?" you can seek out meaning while you are still vital. In the process you will strengthen your links to all that is.

THE MEANING OF THE OTHER

"We are the world," ran a recent pop song, in its struggle to express a spiritual truth. But I noticed that after a vandal in Miami spray-painted those words as graffiti on a bridge, another, wiser, vandal came by and added two more: "part of."

The lyrics might have needed a rewrite, but the intentions of the artists who sang them were good, and an important sign of our culture's maturing. As we develop a new sense of sisterhood and brotherhood, we are, little by little, growing in spirituality.

And state-of-the-art technology is helping to bring that message home. Live satellite coverage of the starving in Ethiopia, and of fundraising concerts in North America, transformed many people's image of humanity.

They began to see themselves not as isolated individuals but as members of the human community—a spiritual concept that rises above our petty differences.

At the same time, some aspects of the environmental movement, such as the fight against acid rain, have begun to appeal to the mainstream of Western society. This reflects the growing belief that we are connected not only with all human beings but with the entire universe, and like gardeners, are entrusted with its well-being.

BECOMING MORE AWARE OF SPIRITUALITY

If you want to become more aware of the spiritual aspect of your personality, here are some guidelines which will help point the way:

1. Ask yourself questions that will provoke a spiritual response. The important thing here is not the right answers. In fact, it is conceivable that you will find no answers at all. The real point of spiritual awareness is to be open to asking the questions.

Anyway, those who claim to have figured out all the answers, whether they are old-time fundamentalists or New Age gurus, are probably kidding themselves.

Becoming a therapist to yourself and to others will lead you to ask such questions as these: "Does my life as a whole have a meaning? Does my day-to-day life show signs of purpose? Given that we will all die and be forgotten, do my relationships with other people and the world really matter? Am I basically loving or basically selfish? Am I satisfied with the way I am living my life?"

2. Give yourself the opportunity to experience inner peace.

There are many ways to help yourself create an island of quiet. You might sit alone in silence, perhaps in the dark, or you might light a candle, and listen to instrumental music that draws your mind deeper.

The frantic rush of many people's lives often means that spiritual awareness is missed by default. We can spend so much time spinning our wheels that we forget to notice where we are going.

3. Spend time with nature.

The city and its technology are not to be shunned. As we've seen, they can provide valuable pathways for the spirit, linking us to the rest of the globe and drawing like-minded people together into community.

But our spirits are also encouraged by wide horizons and water that runs free. The sounds of tree frogs and chickadees can do more to promote inner peace that the rumble of busy streets or the hum of the disk drive.

4. Chose your companions with care.

If you surround yourself with people whose major interest is making money and/or having fun, you will learn little about spirituality from them. Developing friendships with people who grapple from time to time with more fundamental questions will stimulate you to look deeper too.

5. Give of yourself.

How and where you give, whether you give money, time, or energy, is up to you. But this much is clear, giving will provide your spirit with useful exercise, and it's also a pretty reliable test of spiritual health.

CHAPTER TWO

Women and Men

In essence, men and women are alike: walking, talking charac-
ters in a single human drama.

In substance, though, we are diverse. Our bodies, minds, and
emotions are dissimilar in potentially divisive ways. While the
so-called "War of the Sexes" has accentuated those differences
and at times driven us into warring camps, there is another and
better way available to us.

Through understanding our similarities and appreciating our
differences, we can develop deeper friendships across the bound-
ary of the sexes than ever before. Here, almost every statement
about women is by implication about men, and vice versa.

IF WOMEN RULED THE EARTH

There is a recurring discussion around our supper table about
what it would be like if women ruled the earth. Some voices say
the world would be a better place in which to live.

At the least this much seems certain: as women gain more
power, our culture is changing, and for the better. In the past
twenty years, women have made some thrilling leaps in influence
and accomplishment. Little girls today know they can enter
virtually any profession they wish. And as women have actually

entered the ranks of prime ministers and senior executives, the results have been fascinating to watch.

In some cases, they have turned out to be like men-with-skirts, just as capable and clever, just as hard-driving, and just as tolerant of the tyranny of the bottom line. In these cases, while the human race's talent pool has been enlarged, its overall complexion doesn't seem to be much changed.

So when voices around the table argue that more women at the top will automatically make our world a less alienated place, I have to wonder.

On the other hand, in many cases women have brought to the corridors of power a more humane perspective on life itself.

This outlook is based on gentleness, on reverence for other human beings, and on an approach to decision-making based more on co-operation than on the exercise of raw power. And it originates with the core experiences of being female: the vulnerability that accompanies menstruation and pregnancy and the nurturing instincts that develop from the nursing of children.

These important human qualities often go unnoticed thanks to the primacy of the male experience, which in most societies has dominated our idea of what it means to be human. As a result we have created a world in which aggression, competition, and physical strength are the dominant ideals.

Because men don't have experiences corresponding to menstruation, pregnancy, or nursing, this male-dominated world has lacked their "gentling" influence.

But now, as men who are more aware and open-minded recognize how they have been impoverished by an exclusively male perspective, they are welcoming the growing influence of women in our world.

DISCOVERING ASSERTIVENESS

Recently a group of professionals of all ages gathered in a class to learn assertiveness skills. While they were busy practising various useful techniques, their self-understanding was gradually growing alongside their skills, and they discovered that they had two things in common:

1. All of them found it difficult to assert themselves in daily life.

2. All of them were women.

They began to make an important connection: being female automatically made it harder for them to stand up for themselves. In fact, they came to realize that, from childhood on, they had been trained to be "nice" and to be subservient.

As a result, some said they found it absolutely natural to act passive and helpless. Others, attempting to compensate for their diffident tendencies, came across as strident and aggressive.

But in neither group was there anyone who could say that she was comfortable confronting people directly—whether co-workers, supervisors, friends, or husbands.

While the women were often legitimately angry at these people, they gradually began to acknowledge that it was basically their own emotions and attitudes that had been holding them back in life.

For instance, many noted that they don't even attempt to be assertive; they quickly talk themselves out of it, by repeating to themselves tarnished old sayings they were taught in childhood: "It's not ladylike to stand up for myself at work," "I don't have any rights in this situation," "It's my job to keep a man happy," or "My husband is more important than me."

Their excitement began to grow as they put aside these clichés, learned new skills for bringing their feelings to bear on the issues in their lives, and felt their power increase.

Later, back home and at work, they found, thanks to their new, assertive style, that they got a lot of unexpected respect, encouragement, and appreciation from people who like knowing where they stand.

WOMEN AND ANGER

The thing that made it so easy to be around Elizabeth was that she was so pleasant.

Big smile. Lots of white teeth. Elizabeth would do anything for anybody. The last thing anyone suspected was that she was an extremely, deeply, angry person.

Lots of women have difficulty with anger, because they were raised like she was, expected to be nice and smiley, sweet and generous. In some ways, that is the inevitable heritage of a very different age, in which it was more important for women to be nice than to have integrity.

But Elizabeth's sweet smile was just a mask. In reality, her anger snuck out daily, in crooked ways, and one of the major victims was her husband. Crooked anger can show itself in subtle, joking jabs at a person, in dagger looks across a room, or in an overall indifference to people you are expected to love. It can be so subtle that people never know what hit them.

However, they often learn to hit back in self-defence, and Elizabeth, frequently feeling wounded by her husband and other members of her family, came to see that she was making her own life a misery.

Gradually, after five unhappy years of marriage, she began to teach herself how to be straight with others, and how to trust her anger and get it out. It required great courage to abandon her super-sweet approach to life, but, on the other hand, the stakes were high, and she desperately wanted to improve the quality of her relationships.

Talking about her anger came hard enough to Elizabeth, but there was another quite unexpected side effect to this healing process. She found herself crying a lot at the worst times, such as when she was telling her husband that something he did had angered her.

She had always been taught that tears are a sign of weakness, that they detract from legitimate expressions of anger. So at first, whenever she cried, she was tempted to withdraw from the confrontation. Sometimes she even found herself apologizing to him, instead of the other way around.

But through her sobs, Elizabeth began to explain herself to him. "Even though I'm crying," she said, "that doesn't lessen the anger I feel. Whether I'm weeping or not, I want to be taken seriously."

And she was.

STEPHANIE REMAKES HER IMAGE

Stephanie has a major problem. Men are always making passes at her. She literally cannot keep their hands off her body. Sometimes she asks herself, "Why do men keep coming on to me? Am I doing something wrong?"

Take a look at Stephanie. The first thing you might notice are those big, innocent-looking eyes. It takes a lot of careful preening each day to create that deceiving look. In fact it is often impossible to know what her face really looks like, because she wears such a vast amount of make-up.

And with her tight, revealing clothing, she gives the unmistakable impression that she is deliberately trying to be sexy.

Add to the above the fact that she is often flirtatious, and it will not surprise you to know that she is regarded by some men as an accessible body connected to very little brain.

But Stephanie is not what she appears. She is neither dumb nor available. In fact, she is wonderfully bright and creative, and has a lively sense of humour.

And she does not enjoyed getting pawed at by men.

But she is also beginning to recognize that her ideas about her role as a woman are pretty confused. Talking with other women, she is coming to recognize the "come on to me" messages that she sends to males with her makeup and clothing and the way she flirts.

Gradually, she is starting to make some changes, so that her appearance and actions match what is really on her mind.

Of course, it shouldn't really matter how Stephanie looks. Whether or not she fits certain stereotypes, no man has a right to touch a woman's body without her permission. And that self-serving, worn-out, male excuse that she was "just asking for it," simply won't wash anymore.

POWER AND SELF-ESTEEM

Women often feel that they have less power and influence than men. In fact, our society has taught most women from childhood that, for their own safety, they should defer to males and "keep your man happy." In the process, many women have compromised their own legitimate needs, and we, as a culture, male and female, have all been impoverished.

There is no denying that lots of men still think it is wonderful to have women submit to them. But when we examine what that does to their relationships, we discover that they are cheating themselves of companionship and intimacy with women.

An example is the man who asks, "What goes on inside those pretty little heads?" That question itself makes it all too evident that he is afraid to get close enough to uncover the answer. Not only do real men eat quiche, they also possess enough curiosity and courage to find out first-hand what women think.

They are not afraid of women's brains, nor of their strength.

If you are a woman who is fed up with being seen as a "pretty little thing," giving away all your intellectual and emotional power to men, don't wait for their attitudes to alter. The practical truth is that you will probably have to do most of the changing yourself.

The most crucial of your changes will be in the way you regard yourself. It is a simple, if not very flattering, fact that men are less liable to try to take advantage of someone who thinks of herself as valid and powerful. And, of course, those who try it all the same will be less likely to succeed.

So if you rate yourself low in the self-esteem department, if you tend to criticize yourself and to give in too easily to others, do yourself a favour and take every opportunity to develop your own sense of self-worth.

FOUR STEPS TO POWER

Mary Jane made a speech the other day. Afterward, people came up to talk to her, and they told her they experienced her as forceful, strong, and capable. Later she confided to a friend, "They'd all feel different, if they only knew what I'm really like: timid, shy, and unassertive."

"On the other hand," whispered her friend, "maybe you are also that powerful, strong woman they listened to in your speech."

Many people, particularly women, possess far more unused power than they believe they do. So if you would like to increase your own sense of power, here are four steps to take:

First, over the next few days, sit down with pen and paper and make some simple lists. These will form a guide for you over the months to come, so set aside some time for these, and don't scribble them on the backs of envelopes.

Start with a list of the changes you would like to see in your life. Respect you'd like to be given. Relationships you'd like improved. Improvements in your job, whether as homemaker, employee, or employer.

As you write your lists, you will probably find yourself tempted not to set down certain things, because you believe that they are self-indulgent or impossible to achieve. But don't hold back at this stage. It is as important to dream right now as it is to be reasonable. Relax; in time you will be reasonable.

When you are finished, take another piece of paper and list your positive qualities and personality strengths. You are a far more wonderful person than you believe, and this list is going to provide you with incontrovertible proof of that.

The next list may seem like unfamiliar territory. Write down all your rights. For instance, you have the right to have your feelings and opinions respected, the right to physical safety, the right to control your own body, and many other rights. Get them down on paper, no matter how obvious they may seem.

The second step, since it is hard to discover your power in isolation, is to go after some individual support. Find one trusted friend with whom you can check out your lists. He or she is bound to have something to add to what you have written, or something to learn from it.

Third, make it your new policy to surround yourself with people who are committed to growing in assertiveness, strength, and self-esteem. Such people can share your spiritual journey, and dance and laugh with you.

They may or may not constitute a formal group; the crucial thing is only that you let yourself be infected with their zest for growth and hope. Spend more time with this sort of person and less with those who encourage self-doubt.

Fourth, if you are a woman, choose your male companions carefully. There are plenty of "new men" around, men who both enjoy and admire strong women. Such a man will treat you as a valid and valuable partner, and only such a man is worthy of you.

A MOTHERHOOD STATEMENT

As we celebrate the increase in women's self-esteem, their new opportunities, new power, and new careers, it is easy to overlook the experiences of those women who stay at home.

Every day of the year, a mother somewhere is asked, "And what do you do? Do you work?" It is the wrong question, of course.

But some women increase the confusion by replying with the wrong answer. "No, I don't work," they'll say, "I'm just a mother."

There is no such thing as "just" a mother.

True that the human race has been wonderfully enriched by the contributions women are making today in professions previously considered male, but it is a mistake to undervalue the woman who stays away from these more public arenas in order to create an environment in which children can grow up. To its credit, the feminist movement has begun to recognize that caring for children is a way of living out one's womanhood in a very profound and urgent way.

So don't invite the world to under value you. You are not "just" a mother. The only right answer to the wrong question is, "Yes, I work. We all do. I'm a full-time mother."

And if that sounds like a "motherhood statement," that is precisely what I intended.

WOMEN IN THEIR LATE 30s WHO WANT BABIES

Janet, Helen, and Gladys have these three things in common: each of them wants to have a baby, they are all in their mid-thirties, and that biological clock keeps ticking on.

In fact, the trend to later pregnancies has put many women into a battle with time. Janet put off having a baby because she wanted to get her career under way. Helen didn't get married until a couple of years ago. And it was only this year that Gladys and her husband decided for sure that they were ready to be parents.

Helen sees having a child as part of the spiritual meaning of her life. But like Janet and Gladys, she knows that with every year the chances of getting pregnant and having a normal baby decrease. So she is getting very, very anxious.

Before the age of effective contraception, few women had to face this problem. Babies just happened, and mothers coped. Or, in a few cases, they didn't. But now, the twin weights of choice and consequences press very heavily on women's shoulders. They deeply need both an understanding husband and a friend with a good listening ear.

Their fears are many: about their age, about the risks to their baby's health that late pregnancies bring, about the changes that pregnancy will certainly bring to their careers and their marriages. In a sense, if they succeed in becoming pregnant, they will become new people, and there is a great deal of risk to their major relationships in that.

Consequently, the companions they most value are people who are willing to listen in a respectful way as they talk about their fears and the challenges they face.

"Respectful" means keeping an open mind, not having a personal stake in any particular outcome, not taking sides on the issues. It means allowing the women to say what they have to say. Respectful means asking challenging questions, but doing so out of a caring attitude, not to win points.

SINGLE WOMEN WHO WANT TO BE MOTHERS

In our fast-changing society, one of the latest issues to challenge our imagination is the phenomenon of single women who intend to be mothers. I'm particularly intrigued by two questions about them. One is why and the other is how.

There are several reasons why single women are interested in pregnancy. The major factor, of course, is that built-in biological clock which tells a woman she's ready to bear and raise children.

It may be a little humbling for us males, but for some women that urge is quite independent of whether or not there is a man in her life. So single pregnancy can be an important option for a lesbian who wants to raise a child or for a heterosexual woman who is not currently involved with a man or whose marriage has come unstuck.

The how of it is also intriguing. Artificial insemination in a clinic with the sperm of an anonymous stranger, or at home with the sperm of a friend, can take care of the mechanics of conception, but these women face other, more trying issues.

Here are some of the questions they ought to ask themselves:

Should they delay having a child, in the hopes that they will meet the right man before it is too late?

If they have a child now, will that decrease their chance of finding a mate later on?

Might it cause a rift with their parents, friends, or siblings?

Will single parenthood set them back in their careers?

Will it cost more than they can afford?

And, above all, do they have the energy required to raise a child on their own?

There are no obvious or universal answers. In any case, the point is less to find the correct answers than to struggle faithfully with the questions.

THE HAZARDS OF MOTHERHOOD

Every profession has its own "occupational hazards", whether they be physical danger, emotional stress, or disease. But, if you are a mother, your most threatening occupational hazard may well be guilt.

By their very nature, mothers are usually at the centre of the family, constantly watching to make sure that everyone is all right. Because of this, when something goes wrong, too many mothers blame themselves.

If their child gets a cold, or cuts a finger, or drops out of school, or wears strange clothing, or disturbs Father—and all these things tend to happen in family life—then it is guilt that whispers in the mother's ear, "You did something wrong. You should have handled this situation differently. Why didn't you do that instead?"

Adding to the problem, as psychiatry developed in the first half of this century, it got in on the guilt act, blaming mothers for many of the problems their kids experienced, for everything from insecurity to homosexuality.

Today all that has changed. The famous child therapist Dr. Donald Winnicott said it best. He tells mothers they don't have to be any more perfect than anyone else. What he calls "the good-enough mother" is a wonderful presence in a child's life, he says.

So Mother, trust your instincts, forget perfectionism, and, whatever you do, let go of your guilt. That way you will free up more of your natural parenting ability, warmth, and love for your children.

THE MUCH-MALIGNED STEPMOTHER

Stepmothers have never had good press. They are the standard evil characters of many folk and fairy tales, where they supplant good real mothers, like Cinderella's. Eventually, the stories tell us, they are, one and all, defeated by their stepdaughters.

Being a step-anything—stepfather, stepsister, stepbrother—is no bed of roses, and given their reputation, you would think that no one would even dream of becoming a stepmother. But, in fact, the number of stepmothers is on the increase, as old marriages break down and new families spring up.

If you are a stepmother, you have the thorniest job of all. You may be an ordinary human being who happened to fall in love with a man who already has children, but here's a list of demands you have to cope with.

First of all, our society expects a terrific amount of love and labour from mothers, and certainly no less from stepmothers. But loving is never as easy when you don't have that emotional link that comes with raising a child from infancy.

Furthermore, in many cases, your stepchildren will severely test and challenge you, as they would any new person in their lives.

You may have natural children of your own, and at times you are bound to feel torn between their needs and those of your stepchildren. There is only so much of you to go around.

But often the most difficult part is the fact that the memory of the natural mother may still be present in your home. If she died, you may never be able to live up to the idealistic way in which she is remembered. And if she is still alive, the kids may see you as usurping the position she once held.

Of course you are not the wicked stepmother, but, like everyone, you have your limitations. That is why, when you feel stressed-out and over-challenged, when you are tempted to think of yourself as inadequate, it is important to remember that yours is truly one of the world's most demanding jobs. Go easy on yourself.

HELP FOR STEPMOTHERS

To take on a parental role with children who are not your own is never easy. Teachers, visitors to the home, even bus drivers, at times have to discover ways of coping creatively with this challenge.

But the most difficult situation is to be married to, or living with, a parent whose children they once raised with someone else.

Here are three suggestions for stepmothers which will help them and the whole family to build a satisfying life together. With some variations, they are useful for anyone who steps into a parental role.

First of all, recognize that the key to good stepparenting, is not you at all, but the natural father. If he is working with you, supporting you, you will do just fine as a stepmother.

You will have your differences, of course, about issues ranging from food and education to medical care and discipline. That is entirely natural. But what the children need to see is this: when the two of you have come to a decision, you stand together on it.

That way they will know that you are held in high esteem by the father they love. And they will feel secure knowing what the ground rules are, where you stand, and where their dad stands.

Second, don't demand too much of yourself. You may be a loving person, but don't push yourself to adore his children from the very first day. They were raised by someone else, with different values, and they have habits you are not used to. It is almost always a difficult transition.

Finally, don't expect the children will automatically love you either.

Let's face it, you are replacing an important person, or memory, in their lives, and that can hurt a lot. They may need to go through a good deal of grieving, growing, and changing before they are fully ready to accept a new woman in Daddy's life.

So my message is simple: Relax, look to the children's natural parent for support, and don't expect too much too fast.

Remember that, despite what the fairy tales say about wicked stepmothers, your motives are good and his children are lucky to have you in their lives as their *good* stepmother.

THE EMPTY NEST SYNDROME

After Nancy married Richard, in her mid-twenties, she quit her job, gave birth to three children, and put all her energy into raising them.

The next twenty years of her life went by pretty smoothly. She was a contented mother who enjoyed giving herself to her family, until, within a period of two years, all her children suddenly grew up and flew the nest.

Now, with few outside interests to fill her time, Nancy busied herself with the housework. What was once a clean house became immaculate. If Richard so much as moved a cushion, she was right behind him to straighten it up.

One Friday, Nancy's son arrived home for one of his regular visits. Without warning, he marched into the living room, opened his suitcase and strewed clothing, books, and paper from one end of the room to the other.

Then he shouted at his mother that he hated the stifling, antiseptic, compulsive orderliness of the family home.

Shocked and hurt, Nancy thought about the incident that weekend and despite her pain, she realized that, in his devastating way, her son had forced her to see the truth.

It was not long before she registered herself in college and began training to return to the working world. Nowadays, she is more relaxed at home and feels a lot better about her life. Without the aggravation of perfectionism, she and Richard, it goes without saying, are closer than ever.

The moral of the story is that if you are raising children, there is an empty nest in your future. Prepare for it now.

GRAZIE

As a male, I feel a debt of gratitude to the women I have known and worked with over the past two decades. Reflecting on the special gifts of insight that they have given me, I think that many men would echo these ideas in their own words.

This is an age of super-high-technology and hard-nosed budgeting. It is in many ways the time of male triumph, and a reflection of some our best abilities: heady, driving, problem-solving, inventive.

There is some dispute as to whether those qualities have actually done more harm than good to our civilization, but there can be no question at all that they have been extremely hard on our relationships and that some of our most aggressive male achievers have paid for their success by becoming totally burned out.

All this has happened because, traditionally, few males have been encouraged to show any great sensitivity to either relationships or emotions.

On the other hand, women have been consistently curious about what they and we were feeling. Rather than repressing their emotions, they have used them as the means to explore that wonderful inner world of the unconscious mind.

Now the challenge is out to all men to pay attention to our inner, emotional lives, to add a feminine quality to our personalities without obscuring our masculinity.

I am grateful to women for their attention to relationships. While most men will make the effort to pretend that they understand how to maintain an automobile, many continue to act vaguely puzzled about how to maintain a relationship. Too many continue to display, in fact, an absolute lack of curiosity.

Again, women have led the way in paying attention, listening with a sensitive ear to the sounds of the engine of our relationships.

So, in these days of men's technical triumphs, we should be intensely grateful for women's expertise in the two areas most threatened by the hard-driving male world: our emotions and our relationships.

SPECIAL MALE FRIENDSHIPS

When Albert, Marty, Pete, and Sam were first introduced, none of them imagined the change in their lives that would result from that event.

Men often find themselves upset and confused because they are going through major changes in their relationships and careers. This process is usually called the "mid-life crisis"— although it seems to happen these days to males of any age between 28 and 68.

A few years ago, I started a mutual support group for some of these men, and Albert, Marty, Pete, and Sam were among those who began to attend.

All four were successful and creative people, but the special thing about them was how quickly they dropped the typical, protective, male talk about jobs and sports, and really opened up to each other about the changes and confusion in their lives.

Several months later, my summer vacation rolled around, but, somewhat to my surprise, these four kept on meeting—without me. It seems they didn't need me any longer to help them stay honest and open with each other.

And for the past three years, most weeks they have seen each other, as they journey along life's complicated roads. I hear from them that they have their ups and downs together, and I suppose that maybe they won't always be as close.

But the exciting thing to me is that four good men met each other at a deep level, opened up about their problems and their joys, and helped each other along the way.

They became therapists to one another, Albert and Marty and Pete and Sam.

VULNERABILITY, MAN TO MAN

When you think about friendships between men, do the words "vulnerable" or "tender" come to mind? Probably not, because most males keep their friendships pretty distant and cool.

It is true that men are capable of being remarkably tender with women, wonderfully gentle and supportive. But the novelist and theologian Andrew Greeley had it right when he said, "It is a very rare man who is capable of being tender with other men."

Here's how a man we'll call Eric describes his friendships:

"I can joke around with the guys, or discuss sports, or cars, or the stock market. But I don't know how to let down my defences, or talk about the things that really matter to me. I'm actually pretty lonely."

Greeley says that true friendship requires a man to lower his defences and let others see his fragility. This threatens a basic male instinct, for it means risking the possibility that they will hurt him. That's a pretty scary proposition, one which, as Eric recognized, keeps men isolated from the very people who might offer them the most tenderness and understanding.

It remains true that many males find it easier to get support from women, but no woman can truly understand and support a man the way another man can.

So the crucial question is this: can a well-defended, taciturn, powerful male find the courage to become vulnerable with other men?

MEN AND FEELINGS

For many a male, it is a source of quiet pride to hear himself described like this: "One thing you can count on about Bob, he's very even."

"Even" is good. It's level-headed. "Even" holds no troublesome surprises.

So it can come as quite a shock for Bob to hear that his even quality, once a haven of safety, has become a serious problem.

That insight came from his wife, who, after many patient years of observation, angrily pointed out that while his intellectual abilities might be unimpaired, the feeling part of his brain appeared to be uninhabited.

Emotionally, she complained, he was operating at only a fraction of his potential. "I never get any emotion from you," she protested. "You never let me know what you're feeling. You're like a stranger to me."

And then she dropped the bomb: unless Bob decided to do something constructive about the situation, she was on her way out.

Taken aback at first and then shocked out of his complacency, Bob took a look around him at the emotional range of some of the women in his life. He noticed that they could laugh and cry, rage and love, all in the same hour, while on the other hand, his emotional responses, like those of most of the men he knew, hardly ever varied.

For some males the only way to handle a confusing situation like this would be to try more of the same: they would withdraw even further into their shells. But being a wiser, more adventurous soul, Bob started exploring his own life instead, to see if there was any truth to what he was hearing, and, if so, to discover what he could do about it.

He began by asking himself how this came to be, why he felt so even, so emotionally flat. Certainly that was not how his life started. As a baby, like all males, he possessed the same emotional equipment as little girls.

He cried. He laughed. He had temper tantrums. He got scared in the dark. And he reached out in love to his parents.

But when he thought about boyhood, he remembered that certain events had taught him that it wasn't safe to feel or to express his emotions.

Early on, he noticed that his major role model, his dad, kept a pretty firm grip on his emotions. As well, he began to hear that "big boys don't cry," and that those who do are "sissies."

By the time he had been in grade school a while, he imagined he had to act hard and tough, in order to qualify as one of the guys. And pretty soon he had trained himself not to feel anything.

Well, that's the bad news. The good news for Bob was that what males—or females—once learned, they can unlearn. And by deciding to do some unlearning, Bob convinced his wife to give their marriage some more time.

If you are the loving father of a little boy like Bob once was, I have a few suggestions that can make all the difference to how he grows up.

Make sure your son sees you when you are sad or hurt or scared, not just when you are feeling strong or angry.

Make sure he gets a kiss when you come home from work and a chance to sit on your knee and experience your affection.

And even when he becomes a big, husky teenager and there is no way he is going to let you kiss him, you can still make sure you offer him a hug that is more intimate and warm than just a slap on the back.

Imagine the difference, if Bob's dad had been like that.

No, you cannot totally block out the world's influence on your boy, as it evens him out, levels his emotions, flattens his feelings. But with the benefit of your thoughtful and therapeutic fathering, he'll grow up with a much better chance of experiencing the healthy texture of his own emotions.

WHY MEN AVOID EMOTION

There is a popular view that most men have no emotions. But the truth is rather that they rarely show what they are feeling.

Jim and Elaine found it impossible to agree about any topic when they came to see me about their very difficult marriage. But they were unanimous about one thing: Jim showed his wife no feelings, and had rarely even expressed any love or affection for her. Both said that was one of their major problems.

It all seemed pretty clear.

A few days later, however, I saw Jim by himself, and in the safety of our private meeting he described to me the deep emotions, the sadness in particular, that he had been feeling, but had not shown, on the previous visit.

What I concluded was that this apparently tough, unfeeling, cool individual was actually the reverse. In fact, like most of the men I see, he was full of feelings, even though most of the time, as on the previous visit, he showed very little of them to others.

I believe that there are three major reasons that males tend to conceal their deep-down emotions, even from themselves.

The first is genetic. Millions of years ago as hunters, men were programmed, through evolution, to push fears and sadness out of their minds. If you are blinded by the tears in your eyes, how can you hope to escape the sabre-toothed tiger and bring home food to your family?

It is no coincidence that the chemical balance of the male body is high in the hormone androgen, which can cause aggressive behaviour, but low in prolactin, which stimulates the tear glands.

Second, most males were trained as boys to believe that feelings are risky. And as adults they have certainly noticed that the work world rewards males who leave their emotions at home. The good worker is seen as the one who doesn't let his emotions "get in the way of the job."

Third, emotions do, undeniably, rock the boat. Just when a guy is feeling calm, cool, and collected, and enjoying the peace of it all, something unexpected happens which leaves him ruffled, hot, and scattered.

He hears that an old friend has died, and suddenly he's in tears. His child accidentally drops a plate, and suddenly he's screaming at her.

When feeling your feelings is that unsettling, is it any wonder that Jim and other men run from them?

INCENTIVES FOR CHANGE

Men sometimes give the impression that they experience very little emotion. While they may in fact feel more than they are letting on, they often imagine themselves most comfortable when they and others keep the feeling level turned way down low.

After all, that is in many cases the way they were raised. It is what they are used to.

The problem is that the women in their lives can frequently be heard complaining that they are starving for some expression of feeling from their man, dying for a little affection.

While it is perfectly clear that it would mean a lot to their women if they became more emotionally open, most men will still ask themselves the realistic question, What's in it for me?

Here are four solid benefits that any male will appreciate:

The first is that experiencing your emotions can bring a lot more personal satisfaction into your life. If you have ever traded in an old black and white television for a colour set, then you will recognize that almost indescribable sense of seeing everything much more richly.

Too many men still experience their lives in black and white, shades of grey. True, they don't suffer much anger, sadness, or fear. But there is also little happiness or joy in their lives. And no ecstasy.

The second advantage to feeling your emotions is that they give you important information about how you tick: what pleases you, what scares you, what causes tension. People who have good information about themselves have an enormous advantage over the rest of the crowd.

Number three is health. People suffer fewer heart attacks, strokes, and other diseases when they pay attention to how they feel about their personal and work lives, and make changes where necessary.

The fourth advantage is that your love relationships will improve. It is a simple fact that women fall in love with men who feel. If you want to be loved like you haven't been loved for years, get in touch with your emotions. You'll probably become irresistible.

That will put some colour into your life—and your cheeks.

HOW TO EXPERIENCE YOUR EMOTIONS

For men—or women, for that matter—who want to be more in touch with their emotions, there are three essential techniques.

The first is to pay attention to your feelings from time to time. Take a quick inventory of your emotions, for instance, when you are getting up in the morning, when you are at work, or when you are looking at the person you love.

It may help to know that there are four primary "colours" to the emotions: happiness, anger, sadness, and fear. And here's a memory trick to help you recall those primary emotions: their names are "glad," "mad," "sad," and "scared."

In between them there are lots of subtle variations, but if you keep these four in mind, you'll find it easier to chart your feelings.

The second technique is to talk about your feelings. Yes, simply talk.

Just recently a very competent professional found himself stuck in some negative patterns at work that might ultimately have endangered his career. Very tentatively, he started to talk with a friend he trusted about his feelings of fear and guilt, and the more he talked about those feelings, the more he understood the inner ties that were holding him back from success. The more he understood, the freer to succeed he became.

It is no wonder that early psychiatry was nicknamed "the talking cure." Talking really helps with the feelings.

Finally, practise trusting your emotions. For instance, when you feel scared of a situation, maybe that is a good time to withdraw and think things through again, rather than charging in like Rambo.

Trust your feelings, and they will return the favour by providing you with useful information for a happier life.

MEN AND MATURITY

Many men think they want the love of a woman when what they are really after is mother-love. They are still holding onto the old apron strings.

Truth or slander?

A somewhat tongue-in-cheek book by Kenneth Druck described today's male as "the man in the gray flannel pampers."

His point is that, despite appearances, many adult males have not really grown up. In terms of emotional maturity, they are still in diapers.

Sure, they are big and strong, hold down senior positions in management, and all that. They are providers, parents, and politicians. But all that mature-looking stuff is on the surface. Underneath they are still searching for Mother.

In case you are curious about where you stand, here are four questions to help you decide if you are one of the men in the gray flannel pampers.

1. Do you believe in your heart of hearts that your woman should prepare your meals, iron your shirts, and keep the kids out of your hair?

2. Do you think she should look after your social arrangements?

3. Do you believe it is her responsibility to soothe you when you're upset, and take care of your emotional needs?

4. What does the word "tenderness" bring to mind first? The way you treat your woman, or a well-cooked steak?

Those are pretty interesting questions, because few women are really interested in men who have not yet grown up. In the short term, some may be attracted by your prestige and apparent power, but that will soon wear thin and then it can be pretty humiliating to overhear yourself described as emotionally still a baby.

MEN REDISCOVERING STRENGTH

Some men are too gentle for their own good.

Take Henry, for example. He really does have a problem. His employees keep interrupting his work to get help with their own personal projects.

Why, just the other day he was trying to get a few minutes of privacy in a nice way: he quietly, firmly, closed his office door.

But they barged right in.

So Henry hung up a note saying: "Do not disturb." And they went right ahead and disturbed him.

Finally, in utter desperation, poor Henry dragged the couch all the way across his office to block the door—and they tried to push it aside.

Why is this happening?

Well, Henry is one of those fine, sensitive men who are not interested in relying on brute strength and aggression in his relationships. He is trying to find more co-operative ways to work with people.

But being new to all this, he has gradually and unintentionally let go of much of his own, natural, emotional strength and begun to feel almost powerless to assert himself. Threw out the baby with the bathwater.

What a shame. Letting other people push you around is no improvement on your pushing them around. The male as victim is no great improvement on the male as victimizer.

After all, the point of a dynamic life is to meet strength, respectfully, with strength.

But Henry's power is still available. He simply needs exercise. He will have to confront the people who work for him and ask for—demand, if necessary—a little respect.

It's time for Henry to rediscover some of his masculine strength. But of course, before he talks to anyone, he'll have to lug that heavy couch away from his door.

MAINTAINING MALE STRENGTH

As long as men and women have shared this planet, there has been a subtle and shifting power balance between us. That is in the nature of human relationships.

Most recently, men have discovered that the power of the women's liberation movement has liberated them too. The new feminist woman in their lives is not just a playmate and a housekeeper. She is an adult companion.

For any full-blooded male, that arrangement is a whole lot more satisfying. As she was discovering her own strength, he found that he could loosen the reins, share the power, and become more of a free spirit himself.

But while feminism has brought these unexpected rewards to many males, there has been an unexpected, negative side-effect: some men have become pale shadows of their former selves.

Take the case of Stuart. A while back, he and his wife Marie concluded that he had been unfairly dominating their relationship. He made the major decisions, controlled the finances, and frequently scolded his wife for her lack of confidence.

So they started to make some changes.

What they have since discovered, with perfect 20/20 hindsight, is that the reason Stuart dominated Marie was to compensate for his own lifelong lack of self-confidence.

Now, as Marie becomes more dominant, he is starting to wilt like a plant under the hot sun. Fuelled by years of unspoken anger, she no longer hesitates to tell him that he is inadequate, out of touch with his emotions, hopeless at relationships, too quiet, and too boring.

The sad part of it is that he believes her.

Stuart certainly has his faults, and he still has a lot of growing to do. But handing over all this destructive power to Marie is no solution. Stuart was wise to begin to share the power in his marriage, but his task now is to balance Marie's power by paying more attention to his own inner health, by discovering and recovering his self-confidence, his strength, and his pride.

IGNORANCE IS BLISS?

Of all the millions of marriages that are in trouble, the most worrisome are those in which one of the spouses is still trying to deny that there is a crisis going on.

For instance, by the time Jack and Maureen walked into my office for divorce mediation, there was absolutely no question that their marriage was on the rocks. Maureen had walked out on Jack a month ago, had found a new place to live, and had talked with her lawyer about a divorce.

What about Jack? Well, Jack wasn't going to give her a divorce, he said, and he certainly wasn't talking to any lawyer. Somehow this very bright, hard-headed businessman was blinding himself to the most crucial reality in his universe, the fact that he was facing a desperate crisis.

Asking about their marriage, I discovered a consistent pattern—Jack had never paid much attention to their problems. Sure, he noticed that they were growing apart over the years, that their sex life had cooled, and that they didn't confide in each other any more.

"But," he had said to himself, "I guess that's just how it goes."

And three years ago, when Maureen told him she was desperately unhappy, and asked him to go into therapy with her, he got angry, said it was a stupid idea, and buried himself in the newspaper.

This pattern of denial does occur among women, but, frankly, it is much more common among men. And it is a real shame, because if Jack had paid attention to his marriage down through the years, or had responded to Maureen's distress signals three years ago, there is at least an even chance that their relationship could have been saved, and they and their children, family, and friends spared a great deal of pain.

A MESSAGE TO MEN ABOUT CHILD ABUSE

When Pat first arrived at our centre, she was an unhappy, dreary, dried-up, lonely woman, who had somehow misplaced entire decades of her life. By the time she finished working with us, she had become a healthy, vibrant person, with a zest for life.

But the intervening time was intensely painful.

At first, Pat herself did not understand why she was so thoroughly frightened, particularly of men. But as we gave her time and acceptance, long-repressed memories gradually surfaced. They were horrifying.

Pat recalled repeated sexual assaults by a relative while she was a child, and trusted adults who, when she was a teenager, tried to manipulate her into bed.

It took months of immense courage on her part before Pat began to feel some freedom from these memories, to discover her power to resist unwanted attentions, and to trust in her own femininity. It is a mark of her resilient spirit that she persisted throughout these traumatic times, to the point where she began to live again.

Women who have been victims of sexual assault are frequently traumatized just as Pat was. They often suffer from extremely low self-esteem. It is hard for them to trust others, or to endure close relationships. They find it difficult to enjoy sex, even with a loving, understanding partner. And they often become so universally cautious that there is little joy in their lives.

In all this, there are two messages. One is for everyone: that with good support, and plenty of courage and hard work, even very damaged women, like Pat, can recover.

The second message is particularly for men: if you are using children for your own sexual pleasure, you will certainly do them grave damage, and there is a serious risk that you will quite literally ruin their lives.

To any such man I say that, as your own therapist, it's time to recognize that you need outside help with a very dangerous problem.

RAPE IS NOT A WOMEN'S PROBLEM

Most men would agree, if someone happened to ask them, that sexual assault, whether committed against children or adults, is inexcusable. But I believe that we remain far too quiet about our beliefs.

Without intending to, men have given each other the implied message that sexual assault, if not acceptable, is at least tolerable. Let me give you an example.

When the movie *Extremities* with Farah Fawcett first appeared, I attended a screening. The film presents the possibility that a woman who is shrewd, determined, and fit, and—on top of all this—has access to the right tools at the right time, might triumph over even a vicious and determined attempt at sexual assault.

But as the story begins, Fawcett plays a frightened young woman who is being humiliated by a sadistic rapist. At one point he uses some crude wisecracks to terrorize her. And at that point I noticed three young men sitting near me and laughing loudly along with the rapist's remarks.

Why laughing? Well, to be charitable, let's assume they were nervous.

Maybe.

However, the problem is that any potential rapist who had been attracted to the theatre by the topic of the film, might well interpret their laughter as acceptance.

Or tolerance.

Or even support.

Morally, I believe that the clock is running out. It is well past the time for men to make clear to each other exactly where we stand: that rape is not acceptable, and sexual assault is neither tolerable nor humorous.

Women are struggling to take back the night and to defend themselves against rape. They are right to do so. But sexual crimes are essentially a male problem, and only men have the moral power to stop them.

THE HOLISTIC MALE

A recent survey asked 300 women to describe the perfect male. Fully 90 percent said their ideal is the man who is able to be intimate.

Men seem very confused these days about what women want from them. They used to think it was enough to be steady providers or not to drink to excess. Nowadays, some misguided lads try to appeal to women through body building or driving fast cars.

None of it works anymore, if it ever did. The study, conducted by Dr. Lois Davitz, shows that women want what I have often called "the holistic male"—the man who is able to be intimate.

The term "holistic" is a reminder that this kind of man is a balanced, whole person, able to integrate the assertive and action-oriented parts of his personality with the feeling and relating parts. He is an excellent example of the 90-Second Therapist.

Here is a description of how the holistic male handles his relationships, under three simple headings:

First of all, he can talk. About his own inner self and about his feelings. Even if sometimes his defences go way up, he will do his best to get them down again.

Second, he can listen empathically. The holistic male is deeply curious about what's going on beneath the surface of his chosen woman.

Third, he loves her. By "love," I don't mean the clever use of sweet-talk or roses at the crucial moment. I mean that he is committed to her, and to her well-being, in a heart-felt, and if necessary, costly, way.

He also knows he can't buy love, and understands that there is a world of difference between financial expense—"showing a woman a good time"—and making an emotional investment in her.

Women's standards in men are going way up these days, challenging men's age-old expectations and attitudes. They are saying quite clearly that they have never been more ready to give their hearts to the right kind of men.

If, however, the men they meet are not prepared to be intimate—to talk openly, to listen empathically, and to love with their whole hearts—then, these women also say, they are reluctantly willing to do without.

CHAPTER THREE

Love and Sex

We assume that everyone knows how to love. After all, at our most basic, as babies, our love is instinctive. As for sex, males and females possess complementary physical equipment located in approximately the right places.

Love is never that simple, and loving well is quite another matter. There are few teachers of love in the schools of our lives. We learn first and most intensely from our parents, but they are often limited in their love skills.

Besides, because parent-child relationships are distinct from love affairs, they provide us with inherently faulty models. And while, in the best homes at least, our parents may have talked to us about sex, it was impossible for them to demonstrate to us how to be good lovers.

So, ultimately, we must look elsewhere to uncover our society's collected wisdom about love and sex.

THE FOUR C'S OF LOVE

Trying to define "love" is close to impossible, for it grows, unpredictable and wild, like a great tree. Just as you begin to think you have understood its shape, it sprouts another branch.

But there are four words which convey a great deal of its meaning: *contact*, *comfort*, *communication*, and *commitment*.

Love can be the most egotistical and self-centred of experiences, and it can be, at the same time, the most generous and selfless.

When we look at love in terms of contact and comfort, we are talking essentially about the first part, about getting our own needs met.

Contact is being "in touch," simply existing together without thought, without direct communication, perhaps, except for a base emotional response to the other person's voice. This is utterly primitive, the experience of every unborn child safely wrapped in its mother's uterus.

The idea of *comfort* is almost equally primal. This is the soothing warmth of being with the person you love, the entire solution to loneliness. It can be a wonderful source of calm comfort to have a companion, whether to play with as a child or, as an adult, to help pay the rent.

There is absolutely nothing wrong with getting these childlike needs met—far from it—but it is only in the two qualities that complement them, in communication and commitment, that we confront, and, with luck, embrace, our own maturity.

Babies, for instance, *communicate* in only the most primitive ways; they rely on their parents to read their minds and understand their needs. Unfortunately, many people who are chronologically adult also behave that way in their relationships. They never understand why their lives involve constant frustration, as mother/father figures constantly "fail" them.

On the other hand, truly mature, loving people are constantly developing their ability to communicate their ideas and deepest feelings to one another. They are more than willing to risk revealing their vulnerable inner selves for the sake of a satisfying relationship.

Finally, *commitment*. Commitment to the other person's well-being is central to adult love. Mature lovers, intent on their commitment, are always available to their partners and will make great sacrifices for them.

To harken back to that idea of the mighty tree, then, their passion may be seeded in contact and nourished with comfort, but to flourish it must push its roots deep into the dark and fertile ground of communication and commitment.

FALLING IN LOVE IS A CON

One of life's most exciting moments is the beginning of a love affair. The excitement, the sense of discovery, the sheer joy of it all, are among the incomparable highlights of any human being's life.

Some people are so hooked on the experience that they'll say without hesitation, "I hope I never stop falling in love."

But, unknown to them, this powerful experience of strong emotion, to which we have attached the misleading phrase "falling in love," is actually a con job, one of Mother Nature's best, most cunning tricks, elegantly designed so that, no matter what else happens, we will mate and continue the species.

Like a wheel of fortune in a shady gambling joint, the whole thing is fixed. Against this particular proprietor the average citizen doesn't have a chance. She has fixed the game, using sexual feelings so strong that the two people involved can hardly resist tumbling into bed.

Nature devised this experience for one very prosaic and practical reason: human babies are the most helpless of her creations. While newborn fish can feed themselves as soon as they hatch, and mammals instinctively get to their feet and start to walk, our offspring begin by being utterly dependent on their parents.

So Nature's purpose in getting us to fall in love is not only to induce us to make babies, but to create a bond so powerful between lovers that it will hold them together during the time it takes to raise and protect their offspring.

But in her blind commitment to the continuation of the species, Mother Nature overlooks one serious flaw: while "falling in love" successfully drives the couple into the necessary intense involvement, it does nothing at all to guarantee that they are suited to each other or capable of steering their way through a lifetime with each other.

Not only is it like the wheel of fortune, in that it is fixed, falling in love is as random and unreliable as any game of chance when it comes to matching people to each other.

Please don't misunderstand. When people fall in love, a lot of very real things happen. The spring in their steps, the colour in their cheeks, the smiles on their faces, are all undeniable and delightful.

And it may even be love.

But watch out. Mother Nature, in her single-minded devotion to procreation, is certainly up to another clever con, meddling with your emotions for her own ends. Your task is to check out whether you and your partner have the compatibility and commitment to turn the transitory experience of falling in love into a love that can last a lifetime.

FALLING IN LOVE WITH YOUR PARENTS

When people fall in love, the joy they feel is real, the exploration of another's personality is exciting, the sexual feelings are fresh and powerful.

But another, very interesting thing is happening at the same time. They are searching for their parents.

To fall in love is, in some ways, to return to the earliest experiences of infancy. To be cuddled, to be adored, to find, literally or figuratively, a full breast; to be at the centre of someone's universe, just like we were to our parents when we were little.

And our loved one is like a movie screen onto which we can project some of the feelings we might once have directed toward Mom and Dad. For instance, we may say to a lover, "I need you," and that "need" is like the need we had for our parents.

Of course, this very primitive feeling of connection is all part of the glorious experience of falling in love. But it also constitutes the danger.

For when the "falling in love" is over, and the "being in love" is all that is left, those same parental qualities which first attracted us may prove a disaster as our resentment slowly grows.

Then we may see in our lover the control that our parents once exercised over us—or the power, or the judgment, or the anger.

It may, in fact, be an illusion. A lover who is merely assertive may appear to be trying to dominate. A lover who is simply upset may appear to be judgmental. But these echoes of childhood days can bring a love relationship tumbling to the ground.

That is why it is important be aware of what is happening in your unconscious mind as you consciously fall in love. Beware the old song: "I want a girl, just like the girl, who married dear old dad."

The last person you want is to fall in love with is the reflection of your dear old mom or dad.

LOVE AFFAIRS AND BOING!

Most people are overwhelmed when a sexual affair threatens their relationship. Probably the worst part is hearing your partner say that he or she is "falling in love" with somebody new.

But what exactly that confusing little phrase means, nobody seems to know.

Jules Older, a New Zealand family therapist, has made the clever suggestion that we change it a little, just to make its meaning more clear.

He suggests we call it "falling in Boing!"

It's not a bad idea. Try saying it a few times. Notice in particular the way the word Boing! rolls around your tongue and bounces off the sides of your mouth. It's cute, colourful, but not too substantial. Because it lacks the devastating impact of the word "love," it is not nearly so threatening to talk about falling in Boing!

For while falling in Boing! is a wonderful experience, it has only a casual connection with commitment, devotion, or a lifelong relationship.

Boing! has a lot to do with discovering someone new, with adrenalin, and with sexual excitement. It gets lovers thinking about their new romance all day and keeps them awake all night. It gives them boundless energy, makes their skin look good, and puts a spring in their footsteps.

It is absolutely marvellous.

But it isn't love.

So when couples recognize that one of them has merely fallen in Boing! it puts everything into perspective.

Boing! is bounce, like a rubber ball, and given the persistence of gravity, eventually Boing! stops bouncing.

BOING! AND A LONG-LASTING LOVE

When a spouse strays, it may be reassuring to the couple to say that the spouse has merely fallen in Boing!

On the other hand, that phrase may sound a distinctly uncomfortable note to people who, with no strings attached to other relationships, fall in love and hope their love will prove to be long and happy.

For if the Boing! always stops bouncing, they ask, what will they have left?

Here's the good news. Boing! is convertible; given the right conditions, it has the potential to develop into something new and profound.

True, few couples maintain that same breathless excitement they felt when they first fell in love, but many do retain their passion. Not only retain but actually deepen it, adding promise and history to their ardour.

The greatest tragedy in marriage is that so many couples settle for less, once their initial enthusiasm has softened. Their lust gets lost, their passion is past.

No, it is not the loss of Boing! that is to be feared, but the loss of hope, a loss that can be avoided by making a place in their lives where lust and passion can flourish.

REGAINING THE PASSION

Steve and Megan are the kind of warm, relaxed people that folks enjoy having around. If you had asked their friends about their relationship a little while back, they would have replied that, with two children, a lovely home, and a good income, this was one couple who had it made.

No outsider would have guessed that uncertainty about their future together had become the major theme in their relationship. Steve and Megan themselves were totally unaware that a chronic state of anger was leading them inexorably into alienation and frustration.

What they got them thinking was the realization that they not made love for several months. "What's happened to us?" Megan asked her husband one day. "It used to be you couldn't keep your hands off me."

She was right, Steve knew. Like many couples, their courtship and early days of marriage had been superpassionate.

Then it hit them just how long ago that had been. A growing depression settled over them, as they recognized that the beginnings of their sexual problems dated back several years.

Those problems started when the arrival of their children seriously disrupted their old sexual pattern. During the final months of both pregnancies, their feelings tended more toward a desire to protect and nurture the developing baby than toward a passionate need for sex.

And for a while following each birth, they were warned to avoid intercourse as the usual medical precaution.

Nothing out of the ordinary about any of that.

Even after Megan's body had healed, constantly caring for the kids during the day and getting up with them at night left them both too distracted—and frequently too worn out—to resume making love.

Because this is the experience of many parents with young children, they didn't look beyond it.

But although Steve and Megan began eventually to enjoy sex more frequently, they often found themselves anxious about it. It seemed that one wrong word or glance could sometimes ruin the mood and put them off sex again for weeks. What had gone wrong?

Because they both longed to regain the passion they experienced when they first fell in love, they tried talking about their problems, as much as they could understand them, and they both made promises to try harder.

But to their disappointment, there was little improvement, not because they lacked sincerity, but because they had failed all along to recognize the hidden factor that was sabotaging their efforts, the wall of alienation and resentment between them.

In fact, for years Megan and Steve had been sitting on some pretty contentious but unarticulated issues.

To put them briefly, Megan was upset about the increasing time and attention Steve was giving to his very demanding job. And he was harbouring serious doubts about whether Megan cared for him as much as she did her beloved children.

Neither had recognized the impact of these issues on their sexual relationship, or even imagined that they could be related. Both were understandably frightened of rocking their already unstable marriage by discussing them.

At length, desperation itself gave them the courage to face and discuss these insecurities.

The healing process certainly began inauspiciously, as they unleashed bitter complaints about each other's behaviour. Over the weeks, the conflict developed into several angry fights.

Gradually though, the bitterness diminished a little, and the focus shifted, as they began to reassure each other of the depth of their love.

Matching action to their words, Steve started to spend more time with Megan and the family, while Megan arranged a regular babysitter to give the adults some time alone.

Painful though the process was, that's when the glint returned to their eyes and the sexual excitement between them began to flourish again.

Steve and Megan had at length confronted one of our society's best-kept secrets about married life, that anger extinguishes sex just as thoroughly as water does a fire.

SEX: SECRET TO GOOD COUPLE RELATIONSHIPS

Have you noticed how some couples seem especially happy with one another, for reasons that aren't immediately apparent? He may not be handsome; she may not be beautiful. They may not be scintillating conversationalists.

But there is a certain something about them, a sparkle in their eyes, and that something is probably sex.

A happy sex life smooths the bumps, eases the tensions, and keeps the fun alive.

Admittedly, it's easy to enjoy sensational sex during that first passionate crescendo when you are falling in love. The challenge lies in keeping your sexual relationship fun and lively, after years of struggling to build a career, or buy a home, or raise three children.

Here are four suggestions for good sex.

1. Remember that whenever you actually make love, the foreplay begins first thing in the morning. You see, human beings feel much more sexy when they notice that they are cherished by their partners throughout the day. If, at bedtime, you suddenly start paying attention to your lover and touching his or her body, it fools no one.

2. Speaking of bedtime, plan to make love when you're fresh and energetic. Last thing at night, when you're at the end of your energy, is the usual time that people pick. And, in itself, that is enough to explain why many couples have unsatisfactory sex lives.

3. Communicate with each other. Simple phrases such as "I like that," and "More please, over here," can give your partner a much better sense of how to make you happy.

4. Finally, lots of people fall asleep after sex. But as you lie together in the intimate haze that lovers share, don't forget before you drift off, to tell your partner that you love him or her and to say how much you enjoyed making love together today.

24-HOUR-A-DAY FOREPLAY

Although we live surrounded by simulated sex in advertising, films, and magazines, none of it satisfies like the real thing, that natural erotic bond between two people who love each other. In other words, down-to-earth good sex.

And what makes for truly good sex? The answer is 24-hour-a-day foreplay.

That may sound more like an endurance marathon than a turn-on, but look at it this way. In our fast-food society, we have been conditioned to expect instant gratification. Caress the magic button and, presto, instant soup, instant sandwiches, instant information, instant music, instant replay. Why not instant foreplay too?

Without thinking about it, we have come to expect immediate satisfaction in every area of our lives. There are even a few sex manuals which suggest that sex works the same way.

Just rub the right spot at the right speed. Automatic orgasm.

But sex doesn't work like that. It is as natural and fragile as a flower.

While all this may seem self-evident, there are, sadly, a growing number of people who are discovering the hard way that when they ignore or abuse their partners all day, it is almost impossible to interest them in sex at bedtime. No matter what buttons they press, or how cleverly they may caress.

So forget technique. Their partners are looking for attitude.

In short, what "24-hour-a-day foreplay" means is making the entire relationship—day and night, year in and year out—so gentle, kindly, and passionate, that when the moment comes to make love, emotionally you are both more than ready to get turned on.

SELF-ESTEEM IS SEXY

People who get a lot of enjoyment out of their sexual relationship are, almost without exception, those with high self-esteem. They are people who know in their hearts that they are worthwhile and lovable.

These are not the people with good come-ons or great technique, who put their faith in a "dress for success" technique, or who possess that surface-level confidence that borders on arrogance.

No, these are people who possess a quiet, deep belief in themselves.

Their high self-esteem gives them courage to truly open themselves up to another person. They don't hold back because of a fear of self-disclosure.

And since they see themselves in a positive way, it is easy for others to appreciate them too. Self-esteem makes them very, very sexy.

WHAT GOOD SEX DOES FOR YOUR RELATIONSHIP

As oil is to a hinge, so is a good sexual relationship to the life of a couple. It allows everything to move more smoothly, with less effort and fewer squeaks. Here's why.

First, a good love life accomplishes more than just the release of sexual tension. It also helps discharge the stress that builds up naturally in the rough and tumble of every relationship, replacing it with a shared experience of trust and a deep sense of well-being.

As a result, the couple often develop an inner glow which is very attractive.

Second, being naked together helps people become more vulnerable to one another.

Everyone is hurt by others from time to time, and, as a result, many learn to live most of the time with their defences up and their emotions masked, even—or especially—in their most intimate relationships.

Unhappily, those defences keep out not only hurt, but also the emotional warmth that couples most long for.

However, when a committed couple make love together, something magical happens. They shed their defences and their pretences, leaving them on the floor along with their clothing. And then, truly open and vulnerable to each other in their nakedness, they really meet, warmly, wholly.

Finally, sex is the perfect answer to our need to play. The fact that we are no longer children does not mean that we are finished with play. In fact, every adult couple benefits when they exercise the spontaneous and the physical aspects of their nature while tuning out the sedentary and the intellectual.

Most of the time, adults tend to specialize in spectator sports, like watching TV or staring through the windshield.

When we get physically involved in the simple play of good sex, we revive the healthy child within each of us, and that is very good for any relationship.

THE OFFICIAL SEX RULES

The following regulations have never, to my knowledge, been written down before. But according to our research, they have been passed down secretly from mother to daughter, father to son.

Here, in no particular order, we reveal them for the first time:

Rule number 1: Never let your partner see you in the nude. Despite the fitness revolution, the body is shameful. If nudity becomes temporarily unavoidable for some reason, be sure to abstain from frontal exposure. Even in summertime, grab a towel or something opaque. Keep that naked body covered up.

Rule number 2: While having sex, always keep the lights off. No matter how warm the weather, stay under the covers.

Rule number 3: There is only one place to make love: the bedroom. Never the living room, never the kitchen, and never, never, outdoors even if it is entirely private. Think about the neighbors. Think about the mosquitoes.

Rule number 4: Always make love at the proper time: late in the evening when you are too tired to watch the news. Making advances to your partner at any other time may surprise and therefore render him or her vulnerable. All right, maybe in the morning. But never in the afternoon.

Rule number 5: Do not talk with your partner during sex. Too much communication escalates the danger of intimacy and might even increase the risk of enjoyment.

Rule number 6: Never tell your partner what you like or want in sex. If your lover can't read your mind by now, he or she has no right to be in bed with you.

Rule number 7: Do not make loud sounds of any sort, especially sounds of pleasure. It is frivolous, and in any case not at all cool, to be uninhibited.

Rule number 8: The enjoyment of sexual fantasies is bad. If tempted, be sure to stop yourself at once. Useful techniques include thinking about office computers, worrying about the national debt, and planning tomorrow's supper menu. Never share your fantasies with your partner.

Rule number 9: All sex must culminate in intercourse. Penetration spells success. Never fool around just for the fun of it.

Rule number 10: There are a number of terms available to diminish the embarrassment of intimacy. Never use the term "making love." Try "having sex"—it's less personal.

After years spent counselling many hundreds of married couples, I have come to the conclusion that no matter how graphically erotic the images portrayed by popular culture, an entirely different set of values holds sway in the bedrooms of the nation. Our supposedly liberated society has a lot of anxiety about sexual activity.

So break a rule tonight. You'll be a happier couple for it.

THE SEXUAL REVOLUTION IS OUT OF STEAM

Remember the sexual revolution? In the 1960s and 1970s it seemed that everybody was sleeping with everybody else's body. Now, in the late 1980s, there appear to be a few lumps in the mattress.

For instance, recently a young man confided, "With all those diseases out there, I sure don't want to sleep around." That is not the sort of thing you used to hear from men. Before herpes and AIDS hit the headlines, "balling" and "scoring" were the staples of locker room sex talk.

As for young women, they may once have responded to Germaine Greer's pitch for sexual liberation. But today some are listening avidly to her latest message, a call for a return to the traditional virtue of chastity as the modern first line of self-defence.

Another indicator of the change is that the number of virgin females on campus is modestly on the increase, up five percent over six years. One of the reasons is that nowadays their mothers are telling them stories about their own adventures with free love and promiscuity. About how they became more susceptible to cervical cancer, and less fertile, because they slept around and sometimes caught undetected diseases.

But those frightening sexual diseases have only reminded young people of what they suspected all along, that promiscuity is not good for human beings. Those who have experimented with the singles bars and bathhouses affirm that the heart is not likely to flourish in the empty couplings that start there.

Many young people are struggling toward a more profound understanding of their sexual nature. They are not prudes. They believe in the value of physical warmth, and they trust in the goodness of their sexual nature.

But disease aside, some are developing a new maturity, an erotic wisdom, as they recognize the value of not spreading their emotions too thin, not trying to be intimate with everybody who attracts them. They want to give themselves to someone very special.

Their values make good sense, both medically and psychologically.

APPRECIATING YOUR BODY

In order to be considered sexually attractive in our society, people often believe they should possess the perfect body, as defined, of course, by images in the media—whether television, newspaper ads, *Playboy* magazine, or *Vogue*.

"The first thing you need is beautiful hair...." "Cosmetic surgery can work wonders...." "Lose weight naturally...." "The art of looking sensational...." "Thinning hair can ruin the fun in your life...." "Are you too short?..."

But the truth is, very few of us can ever approach the air-brushed perfection of a posed and poised professional model.

That makes people very anxious. Some simply give up, hopelessly deteriorating into drab or flab, while others turn into physique fanatics, frantically pumping iron, or pumping makeup or hairspray.

But there is a third option.

To abandon altogether the artificial media images of physical beauty, and exchange them for something a lot more like you.

Instead of joining the competition, trying to be Mr or Ms Perfect Frame, how about cherishing your own body just the way it is?

Now, it is true that your legs may not be exactly the right length, whatever "right" is, and shape of your nose may be too interesting to fit the preconceptions of an advertising agency.

But let's face it, everyone, even the model, has a bit too much of this or too little of that.

Despite apparent imperfections, you have your own personal grace. Even if you don't seem to measure up against the magazines, in your own individual way, you are beautiful or handsome.

Though it may sound heretical in this world of cellulite wars and thousand-dollar suits, there is something more important still than appearance: no matter how it looks, your body does some pretty wonderful things for you and for your relationships.

Your eyes shine out, announcing the vibrancy of your spirit, while your smile cheers another person's heart.

The warmth emanating from your flesh reminds you of your emotional need for contact, for closeness with other people, and it conveys to your soul the comfort of a touch or a hug.

Your body gives sexual pleasure to the person you make love with and returns pleasure enhanced to you.

Your body, in fact, does you a lot of favours, and asks in return only that you care for it respectfully. Provide it with adequate rest, good food, exercise, and as few irritants as possible, and it will feel so good you won't think about how it looks.

Cherish your body, cherish your self.

KEEPING THE LUST IN A LONG-TERM LOVE

Sex and passion are not only for the young. In fact, when you keep your sexual relationship healthy over the years, it can sustain you wonderfully through those difficult times that every couple experiences, and on into old age.

Many mature people practice the fine art of keeping the lust in a long-term love. You can too.

Do you recall how it pleased you, way back then, when your new-found lover played and flirted with you? Well, you two can still play and flirt together, and as you do, you will find yourself unexpectedly youthful of spirit.

Of course, play comes easier if you create private times together, times when nobody intrudes—not the children, not your work, nobody. Make it an hour, a weekend, or an entire vacation, but be sure you nurture your relationship often.

On such occasions, take a moment to look at each other afresh. In day-to-day life it's easy to treat your partner like a favourite chair which you don't think about, but just expect it to be there. Now is a time to let yourself notice and appreciate your loved one.

If there are times when your desire for each other could be described as "smouldering" rather than "flaming," don't let it worry you unduly; there are seasons like that in every couple's life.

But if the fire does not revive soon, find out why. Here's a hint. The most powerful extinguisher of sexual desire is not, as some folks think, boredom. It's chronic anger. So if something has been upsetting you, don't save it up, talk about it.

Staying open to each other, you will keep the passion flowing. And at the end of your days, the twinkle in your eye will reveal the truth, that you kept the lust in your long-term love.

THE HOLISTIC LOVERS

Certain couples especially appeal to us. We respond instinctively, to the way the threads of their love and sexuality interweave into a life tapestry, which draws our eyes and nourishes our spirits.

Because of their unity, the wholeness we see in their two lives, and their organic connection to their basic nature, we call them the holistic lovers.

The holistic lovers are growing people. They show their affection for each other at every hour, not just when it is time for love-making. They touch without demand. They neither use nor abuse each other.

They communicate frequently about their feelings, fantasies, and desires, whether sexual or not.

Holistic lovers work through their negative experiences and feelings together, so they don't get in the way of their lust for each other. They support each other's self-esteem, and never tear it down through criticism or rejection.

They make themselves vulnerable to each other, both emotionally and physically. And they treat each other's vulnerability with respect and appreciation.

Holistic lovers create an environment for their life together which is as comfortable and inviting as they can manage. They make love in many places, at many different times of day.

They are open to trying new sexual experiences together. They are free to say no to each other. And they know how to say no, without rejecting the other person.

Above all, holistic lovers are people who enjoy saying yes.

PARADOXES OF LOVE

Love is a mystery, ineffable, undefinable. And there is always more to true love than there appears to be.

Love is jealous, even possessive. Yet lovers never yield to their urge to own the beloved. They liberate the one they love, knowing that only when a gift is freely returned is the gift love.

Love is infantile. Like a child at the breast, the lover relaxes, knowing that every need will be supplied. Yet love also encourages the adult within, who will even sacrifice self for the sake of the beloved.

Love is attracted to physical beauty. Yet lovers recognize unconventional beauty, and they see beyond the flesh to the beauty of the spirit.

In the desire to serve the other, the lover appears to lose his or her concern for self. Yet lovers never debase themselves, never count themselves less worthy than their beloved. True love, then, is permeated with self-respect.

Love is two people profoundly at peace with each other. Yet lovers never fear battle, knowing that rage, faced head-on, clears and purifies the air. Love is passionate in more ways than one.

Love makes lovers very powerful. It brightens their eyes, stimulates their energy. Yet in true love, neither is stronger than the other. When it comes to their hearts, the two are equal.

And their love is never more perfect than when they are entirely vulnerable to each other.

CHAPTER FOUR

Successful Relationships

In relationships, we learn to offer ourselves as gifts to each other, and to receive each other as treasure. Whether our relationships are as children, parents, friends, lovers, spouses, professionals, or colleagues, their common role is to wean our spirits away from self-involvement, to challenge and to nurture us.

RELATIONSHIPS

Our relationships are as fragile as cobweb and as tough as rawhide.

They form the inescapable environment which surrounds even the most isolated persons. Even the hermit, voluntarily isolated from others, lives alone in a vain attempt to escape troubled, still-living memories of childhood, family, and friends.

And for those who appear to sleep alone, relationships provide the plot of each night's dream life.

Our need for relationships is as primitive as eating and breathing. They provide the context within which we nurture our young, make love and make lust, struggle for power, create our life works. Complemented by wisdom and endurance, they may carry us through the roughest weather.

In short, there is nothing of significance in human life which does not depend upon our relationships.

And when we depart, a question: do we die alone, or do the personalities of those we love somehow shelter and accompany us on our way?

THE QUALITIES OF FRIENDSHIP

When life is stormy and lonely, the finest, safest haven is true friendship.

True friendship is rare. Despite our many acquaintances, there are few people with whom we are deeply intimate. And yet friendship is essential to our humanity.

Friendship costs. It demands time, honesty, and vulnerability. And that is why, I'm afraid, friendship is rarer among men than among women; men often lack the self-confidence to let down their defenses.

Because a true friend gets a lot from the relationship, he or she can afford to be generous. Your friend will never betray you—not for love and not for money.

Whether in the same room or on another continent, whether your moods are up or down, your true friend really wants to listen. And hearing your story is never an excuse to say, "Oh, that reminds me...."

Though your friend knows the darkest corners of your personality, he or she never forgets your best qualities and your kindest acts. So you never have to lie to your friend, and your friend never has to make destructive judgments.

And yet, paradoxically, it is your friend who has the courage to challenge you when you are off-base, while acquaintances and family may just stand back and let you do your own thing.

Your friend may be a co-worker, a partner in sports, or your spouse. While acquaintances come and go, this true friend is irreplaceable.

A FRIEND IN NEED...

It was the day after John and his wife separated. A week before, he had made plans to bowl with his two best friends. Having decided not to sit around and mope, he kept the date, but said nothing to them about his marriage, and bowled badly. Disastrously, in fact; he could hardly keep the ball out of the gutter.

Afterward, over a beer, he got around to telling his friends the reason he had achieved such a low score.

This is how they responded:

Jason: "Oh well, anyone can have a bad night," then silence.

And Mark, "I never know what to say at times like this."

Period.

Next topic.

Football scores.

Later, hurt and disappointed, John wondered why his friends turned out to be so unhelpful.

Part of the problem may have been John himself. Perhaps the evening would have ended differently if he had been more up front with his friends, let them know how he felt. "Look, guys, I don't feel much like bowling tonight. Marg and I split up yesterday, and I'm pretty shaky. What would you say about going somewhere where we can talk?"

The other half of the problem, though, is exactly the way Mark explained it. I like his awkward honesty, admitting that he doesn't know how to respond to people who are hurting.

This is for Mark, Jason, and everyone else who cares. If you're not the kind of person who wants to disappoint someone who is already hurting, here are simple guidelines for being a good friend, in times of need.

First of all, these three simple phrases that will mean a lot to your friend: "I'm really sorry to hear about that," "Is there anything I can do?" and, especially, "Would you like to talk some more about it?"

Count on it, even your most poker-faced friend has many more emotions below the surface than he or she is showing. Your friend will find it a great relief to know there is someone around who is willing to listen.

The second guideline is simply that: listen.

You don't have to solve problems. You don't have to find solutions. You don't have to be Sigmund Freud. Just sit or stand or walk with your friend, and hear what he or she has to say. Simple responses like, "Uh-huh," "Really?" "I can imagine," and "Tell me more," are all you will need to keep the conversation going. No clever answers required.

The third guideline is, don't be scared off if your friend gets into heavy feelings—deep sorrow, fear, or even anger. None of them will hurt you. And there is nothing you have to do about them. Just listen. The kindest thing you can do is to let your friend be, just be, the way he or she is right now.

The fourth guideline is to make time for your friend. That extra lunch hour or evening together during this tough phase will mean a lot. Even a five-minute phone call that begins, "Hi, I wondered how you're feeling today," can be a great lift to someone who's struggling through the valley of the shadow. It tells your friend that there is someone out there who cares.

The fifth guideline is hope.

Hope is not, "Cheer up. Don't be gloomy. It's all going to be fine."

Hope is, "I believe in you. I know that when you are finished with feeling this necessary misery, you are going to be fine." Hope is being willing to wait for the healing.

By hoping for your friend, you become part of the healing.

THE RISK IN GOOD FRIENDSHIP

The silence of a life without friendship can be deafening. Unlikely as it may seem, those who lead busy, crowded lives can, in fact, be trapped in lonely solitude.

Someone who knows about this first-hand is Olivia. Listen to her description of herself: "I've got lots of acquaintances. But I have no true friends, not one soul I can really confide in."

What keeps her many associates from developing into a true friends is the fact that she and they rarely open themselves up to each other.

They lack the key to friendship, which is vulnerability. People who are vulnerable to each other are willing to talk about the hidden corners of their lives, and will allow their friend to see them in their shakiest moments.

"Easy to say," you may reply, "but not so simple to do." And you are right, of course.

"If I let it all hang out," you worry, "this person might think I'm an idiot. Or gossip about me. Or stab me in the back. No way am I opening up."

And yet, that is exactly what friendship is about. It is taking the very frightening risk that you might be hurt.

Such is the essential nature of the human personality that this quality of vulnerability is the only way to experience true friendship.

On the other hand, you do have a safety net. You won't open up unless you have reason to trust the person you are with.

Sensible people don't lie down in front of locomotives, and they don't make themselves vulnerable to bullies, gossips, or self-centred egotists. They are choosy about their friendships, classy about their demands.

But their bottom line is this: "I need solid, deep friendships. If that requires vulnerability, then so be it. It's worth the risk."

MACHO INTIMACY

The macho approach to life, a by-product of the still-adolescent quality of our culture, suggests that the best way to deal with problems of a troubled world is to "hang in there" silently and "tough it out," rather than trying to change destructive structures imaginatively.

In the more private world of relationships and the inner life, the solution to unhappiness is the same: "Tough it out," say macho lovers. Don't experiment with a new approach, don't talk about it.

Simply hang in, and maybe something will get better all by itself.

What attracts them to this strategy is that, in the short term, it works. Or, to be more precise, sort-of-works. You can ignore heartache—for a while. You can co-exist at home with someone you don't get along with—for a while.

In the long term, though, when you ignore genuine difficulties, they rarely go away, whether in politics or intimate relationships.

Unfortunately, the proponents of emotional machismo rarely possess sufficient interpersonal skills to sustain them in their self-imposed isolation. So many of those who tough it out end up with broken relationships, a variety of stress-related physical illnesses, and, at the emotional level, anxiety and depression.

Those who live to the fullest are of an entirely different sort—it takes imagination, initiative, strength, and courage to face problems head-on.

90-Second Therapists are more honest with themselves and more motivated to develop their potential. I'm sure it's obvious, but I admire them enormously.

THE MAGIC POWERS OF TOUCHING

Within the next couple of hours, the chances are you will find yourself close to someone you like, or love, a lot. The question is, will you touch them?

Sometimes we figure that adults don't need touch, except maybe as a prelude to sex. We tend to forget that gentle, undemanding touch has a wonderful power to comfort, to reassure, and to heal.

Recently I watched a television feature about a hospital nursery for newborn babies who aren't yet ready to go home with their mothers. The hospital provides volunteers to make sure these infants get their share of being touched and held. One of the volunteers is an elderly male security guard, who, in his off-hours, visits the hospital just to cuddle these tiny babies and murmur little nothings to them like an affectionate parent.

Well, we all know that it is good for babies to be touched, that it stimulates their growth, emotionally and even intellectually.

However, we sometimes don't recognize that it is also good for adults, even elderly male security guards. In fact, it is good for all of us to be involved in the physical nurturing of children.

The old man said it best, though. Beaming with delight at the camera, he explained, "You don't know who is cuddling who."

A popular bumper sticker from a decade ago asked, "Have you hugged your kids today?" The assumption was that kids need to be touched, and they do.

The truth is, however, adults need those hugs every bit as much.

DOES ABSENCE MAKE THE HEART GROW FONDER?

Arthur's monthly phone bills look like mortgage payments.

He and his lover live hundreds of miles apart. But despite the staggering expense of maintaining their long-distance relationship, he seems very happy.

The number of long-distance love affairs is on the increase because people are very mobile these days, and relatively well-off. And, as Arthur points out, absence really does make his heart grow fonder.

One of the strengths of these relationships is that such couples are not relying entirely on sexual gratification to hold them together. Arthur's relationship is also nourished by an intellectual and emotional excitement that can be sustained by letter and telephone.

Another plus is that people who handle a long-distance affair well are good at tolerating delayed gratification. That tends to make them more reliable in the long haul, which, should they ever decide to live together, can be a pretty useful talent.

But there is also a down side. The very fact that the couple meets less often may keep a romantic gloss on the relationship, but in the rough and tumble of sharing a home, that artificial shine might wear off sooner.

Unless they do move in together, they will never know whether they can maintain the passion.

But then, that is the unknown all of us must face, whenever we travel the long distance from loving together to living together.

ASSERTIVENESS OR AGGRESSION?

How often have you kicked yourself because you let someone else push you around? If your answer is "Too often," then it is time for you to become more assertive.

But what exactly does assertive mean?

The three essential words in the assertiveness vocabulary are "passive," "aggressive," and, of course, "assertive." Few people have any difficulty understanding the word "passive."

Passive means letting others walk all over you, either because you don't care much, or you have such low self-esteem that you don't believe you deserve the best, or you simply do not possess the skills to be assertive.

In any case, as most people recognize, passive is trouble.

What is often less clear is how "assertive" is different from "aggressive." After all, both terms have a fair amount of "push" to them. But aggressive behaviour, like passive behaviour, is often based on low self-esteem. Aggressive people push in a rough, uncaring way because they don't feel confident. Not daring to hope that people will give them what is rightfully theirs, they believe they have to grab for it.

Like passive behaviour, it is often born of desperation. It is certainly not an attractive style, nor one which promotes good relationships.

That brings us to assertiveness.

Assertiveness is based on a sense of self-worth. Assertive people ask for what they need, knowing that they deserve to be treated respectfully. Assertive people push where necessary, but with respect for the rights of others. They live with the basic expectation that life will be good.

Still, many folks find the terms confusing. In fact, they fear that if they are assertive, they will be seen as being like those insensitive people who are always shoving others around.

And, naturally enough, they fear loss. Assertiveness, they worry, may lead to rejection.

But being assertive actually has the opposite effect. Because you ask for what you want, people know what to expect from you. Because you refuse requests that are unreasonable, they learn to respect you.

And because you don't let yourself be treated like a doormat, they never become used to walking all over you. They see you as you are, as a real person, who, when you're treated right, has lots of warmth to share.

As they come to understand that, they'll appreciate you all the more for being assertive.

WOMEN AND PASSIVITY

Margaret used to complain that everybody took advantage of her. At the office, her boss gave her twice as much work as anyone else, and when she arrived home exhausted, her husband expected her to wait on him hand and foot.

She often sighed that she could not understand why people were so thoughtless.

In fact, there were two possible explanations. Either her boss and her husband were totally insensitive, or she had no idea of how to be assertive with them.

In fact, probably both were partially true. But since the boss and husband are out of our reach, let's deal with Margaret.

Passivity is a very common problem for women like Margaret. Typically, they grew up in families with an unassertive mother as their major role model, while men like Dad were supposed to be "on top of things" and "in control." Margaret's brothers, like Dad, were expected to be aggressive, to make sure no one pushed them around, and to play rough sports.

Girls, on the other hand, were to be compliant, to do as they were told, and to help keep the household running. In relationships they were expected to be passive. At least, that is the message that Margaret got from Mom and Dad.

But passive people—whether male or female—almost always grow up like Margaret, being used and abused, and if they are at all healthy, they are eventually bound to resent it.

They become sulky, they turn snappy, and they may start manipulating. They do nothing which would be seen as openly defiant, nothing which invites overt anger. But they are the sort of people who consistently show up late for appointments, or who subtly reject their spouses and make sly digs about them in public.

Because there is a belligerent undercurrent to their behaviour, a sense of "I'm going to get you back for all this abuse," their character has aptly been described as "passive-aggressive."

Not a very appealing picture, but there is a happy footnote to this description.

As Margaret began to practise some basic assertiveness skills, she discovered two important facts. First, she could change her attitudes; since she didn't have to see herself as a victim, she didn't have to play victim. Consequently, she was less angry more of the time.

Second, by changing her attitudes, she could actually change her environment. As she developed a firmer stance, her worklife and her marriage actually improved. Through assertiveness, she began to enjoy life in ways she had never guessed possible.

FIRST STEPS TO ASSERTIVENESS

Assertiveness training courses can be a lot of fun for everyone. The participants generally have a fine time rediscovering strengths they haven't used for a long time, while the leaders have the pleasure of helping formerly repressed people become more fully alive, all within a couple of days.

In the best courses, the students experience both a private inner journey, in which they come to terms with those aspects of their personal history which hold them back from self-assertion, and an opportunity to go public as they practise new styles of communication with others.

If you'd like to take an assertiveness course of your own design, here are three easy techniques to get you started.

First, sit down by yourself with a pen and paper and take an objective look at your own behaviour. Remembering that you don't have to show this to anyone, answer these questions as honestly as you can:

"Looking back over the past week, how do I feel about my relationships with others? Looking at them from an assertiveness point of view, would I class myself as passive, aggressive, or assertive? If I met me on the street or at a party, would I think I was too compliant for my own good? If I am passive or aggressive, does that cost others?"

Next, as soon as you can find another quiet half-hour, write yourself a letter. Begin it with these words: "Here is how I would like to be treated by others...." Keep writing until you feel it is complete.

Once you have that part clear—asserting your wishes to yourself—you will find that asking them of others, out loud, will feel a whole lot easier.

The third step is to experiment with assertion. Here the key to success is to start small. For instance, many people find it easier to be assertive with children than with adults, with strangers than with friends, with neighbours than with parents, with co-workers than with spouses.

Begin where you feel most comfortable, and you are more likely to experience success. Score even a few minor successes and you will find yourself ready to take some risks with the more threatening people in your life.

Does the thought of being more assertive make you anxious? Don't worry, you are not alone. But believe me, by the second or third time you stand up for yourself and for what you believe in, you will find your anxiety decreasing and your self-esteem on the ascent.

Because assertiveness is becoming a way of life now, you will also begin to notice that you are not alone. Rather you are surrounded by people who, in thoughtful and kind ways, make certain that others treat them with respect.

INTIMACY AND ANGER

Least said, soonest mended.

It makes sense, doesn't it? No angry words, so no hard feelings. Our culture seems to have a lot of respect for that old proverb. But it doesn't always work.

Recently Daniel found he was having great difficulty maintaining an intimate relationship. The basic problem was that every time he became angry with the woman he loved, Daniel would withdraw from her. For many long days at a time, he would have nothing at all to say to her.

Of course, she gradually became fed up with this silence-that-was-supposed-to-be-a-relationship and found herself on the point of leaving him.

What turned this near-disaster into something positive was Daniel's curiosity. Wondering to himself why he kept withdrawing, he suddenly remembered something quite important, that proverb his parents had repeated to him so often as a child: "Least said, soonest mended."

Now the saying does have a limited amount of surface logic. If you don't say too much in an argument, maybe you won't hurt anyone's feelings, and theoretically the relationship should mend quickly.

Unfortunately, the reality is that usually nothing gets mended, while the relationship festers and gets worse.

In fact, when Daniel was a child, his parents were both chronically afraid of anger. Learning about life from their example, as children always do, he became so fearful of his own rage that, as an adult, he was, ironically destroying his relationship in order to save it.

In many families, such apparently wise sayings conceal a crippling fear of intimacy. For intimacy requires honest anger as much as it requires more conventional virtues like gentleness and kindness.

Let there be no confusion. There is absolutely no justification for abusiveness, whether physical or emotional. But abuse was not Daniel's problem.

Contrary to the proverb, learning to say, "I'm angry, and here's why," as Daniel did, can be a profound and loving contribution to a happy relationship.

OPPOSITES ATTRACT—CAN THEY LIVE TOGETHER?

One of the best, and the worst, things about friendships and family is the fact that everyone is so different from everyone else. Human beings occur in nature with an infinite variety of personalities, not one of us like any other.

Some are introverts, some, extroverts. Some tend to think, while others tend to feel. Some have their minds made up already, while others are still looking around to see what's what. Some make decisions intuitively, while others think things through rationally.

The most creative response to this diversity is "Vive la difference." Let's enjoy the ways that we are different. In fact, let's appreciate how those differences actually enrich us.

An example. If you like to save money, and your partner's motto is "Born To Shop," you two are very different in fairly important ways. So you may be tempted to waste your energy by trying to make the other into a carbon copy of yourself.

In fact, you have a choice. You can turn those differences into a source of tension, each criticizing and putting down the other. Or the two of you can learn to look to each other as examples of the infinite possibilities of the human personality.

You who are frugal, almost to the point of boredom, can learn from your companion how to loosen up and have some fun, while the spendthrift can learn from you to exercise a little caution, to think more about tomorrow.

Another common example. One of you may be a high-flying optimist. Your approach is, relax. It's all going to work out fine. The other may be Murphy's Law personified. If something can go wrong, it will.

Again, you could spend a lifetime—and a thoroughly miserable lifetime at that—fighting about whose approach is right. The irony, however, is that to a certain extent you are both right.

It could be a lot more satisfying instead to learn to appreciate the unique qualities that the other brings to your relationship. After all, one of the reasons that human beings gravitate into twos is that a couple has more innate strength to cope with a complex world than one person alone.

Couples, then, are doubly effective when they have the capacity both to foresee problems and to enjoy the moment.

If you can appreciate the qualities in your loved ones that are not like your own, not only will you learn some important lessons about life from them, you are also likely to enjoy it more, together.

CHAPTER FIVE

Your Own Premarital Course

Are you getting married? As you plan to link your two lives formally, it is urgent that you take a penetrating look at what this new commitment will mean to you and at the kind of lifestyle you hope will result.

You might answer that you simply want to be "together, forever, and don't confuse me with questions." Well, there is nothing unnatural about that attitude. It's the same single-minded urge that propels most couples into marriage, and it's a wonderful feeling. But being "together, forever," will bring with it consequences as yet unforeseen, maybe more complicated than you imagine, and certainly far more complex than for previous generations.

In their rush to the altar (or city hall), in their concentration on planning a beautiful wedding rather than a lasting marriage, many couples remain sadly oblivious to questions which could help them avoid years of discomfort. So, if you believe that your relationship deserves the best start it can get, and if you want to avoid pitfalls that break up even good relationships, spend some time together with the ideas and questions that follow.

YOUR OWN PREMARITAL COURSE

If you have read this far, you are probably the kind of couple who would appreciate attending a marriage preparation course, meeting others at the same stage of life, and talking about the hopes and the challenges of this special time in your life.

But if you are unable to attend an organized class, here is an outline for your own personal marriage preparation course, to help you prepare for the changes you are facing. Read through this outline together, and talk about it, and you will find you have at least touched most of the bases.

Keep in mind that, no matter how well you two know each other, with every major change in your lives together, you will get reacquainted in a different way. Making a commitment and living together is one such change, and so, if some of your discussions take you way out into left field, trust the process and see what you learn about each other out there.

THE CHANGING FACE OF MARRIAGE PREPARATION

During the past decade, there has been a significant change in the interests of couples attending marriage preparation courses.

They used to be, almost without exception, between the ages of 18 and 25. More often than not, they arrived not because they had a driving urge to prepare themselves, but because their priest or minister had insisted they attend. Their experience of life was often limited, and they gave the impression that they had the world by the tail.

So, although unfailingly polite to their earnest instructors, they were not much interested in their central message, that high-quality communication and sophisticated conflict resolution can keep relationships healthy. In fact, generally these couples seemed to think that their communication was "fine, thank you," and conflict was a problem other people suffered from.

In recent years, the proportion of older couples attending these courses has increased dramatically, and in some cases they are preparing for a second marriage. These couples attend because they like the idea of sharing their hopes and questions with a group of others who are involved in the same exciting process. They have enough life experience to know that for their marriages to survive, they have to get a good start.

They want to learn from their mistakes in the past. They are often very open about the failures in communication which led to the breakdown of former relationships. And they are more curious than ever about the positive values of conflict.

Our society's growing sophistication about what makes relationships work well, along with the obvious number of marriages in distress, is reminding couples of all ages to prepare carefully for the challenge of life together.

COMMUNICATION

Communication is the key to a happy relationship. Whether by a word, a silence, a touch, or a look, you communicate volumes every day.

Pay attention to your communication patterns. Do you actually say what you most want to say to each other? Do you hear each other clearly? What keeps you from communicating? Did your parents communicate well when you were young? If not, have you picked up any of their bad habits?

CONFLICT

Conflict is a special kind of communication, one which helps you two get to know each other better, and create patterns of living together which you can both enjoy.

Does conflict scare you? Do you two know how to fight fair and clean? Are you growing in your ability to resolve disputes as a couple? Have previous relationships left you with scars which will affect this new relationship?

SEX AND FAMILY

Have you talked about what sex means to each of you? Have you planned whether and how to have a family? Are you up to date on the various methods of contraception, their merits and defects?

Do you like children? Have you spent much time with other people's kids? If you were to relive your own childhood, what would you change?

ROLES

Are the two of you aware of the roles you expect each other to assume? Are stereotyped sex-roles likely to trip you up? To cite the most typical example, he slaves at the office to support the family financially, while she slaves at home to create a perfect home for the family. And both resent it.

Make sure you give close attention to the most dangerous hot spots: Who is going to take care of the children, the car, the housework, the finances? Whose career is most important? Who is responsible for saying "I love you" first. Who is expected to initiate love-making?

Beware of easy answers like, "We'll share it." The reality is that one of you will be better at certain things, and in some cases that person will end up doing them. How will you keep the balance fair? How will you keep yourselves from hardening into rigid roles, and subsequent resentment, which are based on your being either male or female. Do you intend to keep checking with each other?

And what if today's answers change tomorrow?

EXPECTATIONS

Make sure you know what your expectations are. Many couples flounder not because of having differing views on crucial issues, but because they don't recognize ahead of time how much they differ.

Do you agree on whether and when to have children, what kind of home and lifestyle you want, how you will spend your money, the relative importance of family and your careers, the place of religion in your lives, the status of each other's relatives and friends, and (not as obvious a question as it once was) how long you expect this marriage to last?

Assume that you will have differing responses to at least some of these questions. What now? How can you prepare for the inevitable conflicts?

CHANGE

Have you talked together about the fact that both of you will change as the weeks and years roll by? You can't predict exactly how you will change, how your attitudes and feelings may shift, but you should have a few clues. Have you recognized together that change can be one of your greatest assets as you grow through life?

LEGALITIES

Do you understand the legal ramifications of marriage, whether formalized or common-law? Would a talk with a lawyer, or the writing of a marriage contract, help you to clarify and formalize your intentions?

Remember that marriage contracts are inherently limited in what they can accomplish but they can force you to ask yourselves a lot of important questions about your marriage, particularly regarding finances, and help you clarify what will happen if either of you should die prematurely or the marriage break up.

On the other hand, even if a contract attempts to deal with the more troublesome day-to-day issues, providing for instance that you will both share in the dishwashing, you may not be inclined to have the courts enforce it every time your spouse turns on the TV after supper. Again, how will you deal with conflict?

STRATEGIES TO AVOID DEALING WITH PROBLEMS

Therapists and other wise guys are always saying that you have to face up to the inevitable problems in your relationship. Deal with your conflict, they nag, learn to communicate better, and so on.

Let's face it, millions of people use other strategies. For instance, at times of stress they may distract themselves by having babies, putting an extension on the house, starting a new business, having an affair, or learning Scottish country dancing.

People will do anything that's legal, and a few things that aren't, to avoid dealing with the problems in their relationships.

These strategies themselves involve, of course, one small but unavoidable problem: eventually you may run out of babies, extensions, businesses, lovers, and Scots.

What will hold you together then?

PUTTING YOUR BEST FACE FORWARD

It is cynical but true to say that when you woo someone, you are engaged in a marketing operation. You want your beloved to see you in the most attractive light possible, so he or she will feel attracted to you.

As a lover, you probably put on your best face when you are courting. Even though you don't intend to mislead the other, you do try to sell yourself. You do this in all innocence, of course, but watchful consumer advocates would probably classify this practise as false advertising and/or misleading packaging.

However, after you marry or start living together, you may find that your clever marketing face keeps slipping off despite your best efforts, and your carefully packaged personality gets opened. Within the intimacy of marriage every facet of your true self must ultimately be revealed, and some of those alluring images of early courtship can never survive the rigours of real life.

Occasionally, that marketing face doesn't even survive the honeymoon. New spouses have been shocked to find that by the day after the wedding, their attentive, sweet, generous, and concerned lover has turned into a moody, self-involved, and angry enemy agent.

One useful tactic to check how honest you and your beloved have been with one another ahead of time is for each of you privately to take The Secrets Test.

THE SECRETS TEST

1. Do you have any secrets about your family's history that you have kept from your partner?

2. Are there any secrets from your own personal past which you have held back?

3. Do you have any personal quirks or habits that your partner probably doesn't know about yet?

4. Are there other aspects of your personality which you are frightened to let your partner see?

5. Have you noticed yourself putting some effort into keeping those things quiet, at least until the wedding is over?

6. Are there questions about your partner's own history or personality which concern you, but which you haven't yet asked about?

7. Are there things about his or her personality which bother you but which you have never dared mention?

8. Do you have hopes or expectations for your marriage which you haven't talked about together?

At our Toronto Centre for the Family, we suggest that partners not show each other their actual answers, but treat them as personal information which can stimulate a variety of honest conversations.

We have administered this questionnaire to hundreds of couples about to start a life together. In any group, there are likely to be at least a few "Yes" answers in every category.

However, the most common areas of secrecy are those touched on in questions 2, 3, and 7. If you are like many of our respondents, you may hesitate to talk openly about your past secrets, or about your own quirks and habits, and you may also be anxious about discussing your partner's disturbing personality traits.

Take courage and give yourself a break. For the sake of your future together, if you have things to talk about, talk about them now. Don't wait until after all the commitments have been made, because by then the issues may have been clouded over by resentment about being sold a bill of goods.

MORE ABOUT CONFLICT

Or, "You can't make an omelette without breaking eggs."

There are various ways of handling conflict. They include screaming or throwing things, sweeping it all under the rug, distracting yourself from noticing, and using the silent treatment.

On the other hand, you can deal with conflict face to face.

CONFLICT AND THE BRIDE AND GROOM

Here are four important messages about conflict for couples contemplating living together.

1. Intimacy is impossible without conflict.

You hate conflict, right?

Well, learn to love it; for those who put a lid on their conflict will eventually find they have inadvertently put a lid on their ecstasy. And although intimacy is the goal most people have for their relationships, conflict-free couples tend to experience the exact opposite: distant, flat, and disappointing marriages.

2. Conflict is inevitable in any intimate relationship.

By my admittedly perverse definition, life in a couple consists of two people squeezed into a space designed for only one. So don't be scared off by conflict. You are engaged in making space in your life for another human being who has sharp knees and elbows.

You would have to be either pretty dull or desperately intimidated not to make waves sometimes.

3. Conflict is a way to learn about the other and about yourself.

When you are in conflict, you listen first to yourself and discover more about what hurts your feelings or crowds your space. And as you listen to your partner in the midst of a fight, you discover something authentic about him or her that those long moonlit talks might by themselves have never explained.

4. There are good ways to handle conflict and there are bad ways.

If you learn the constructive ways to use conflict, your relationship is likely to be sensational. Good conflict skills are not hard to learn. All it takes is commitment.

KEY CONFLICT STRATEGIES FOR NEW COUPLES

Remember these crucial points:

1. Don't bury conflict.

Hidden anger goes underground and burns people in the most unexpected ways. Talk together about everything that isn't going well in your relationship.

2. Don't throw in the kitchen sink.

If you're in conflict about, say, your partner's rude manners, stick with that topic. Now is not the time to discuss his or her grooming, choice of companions, or academic record. Enough is enough.

3. Try to talk about your feelings, rather than about the other person's defects.

For instance, "I feel scared when you yell at me," is much more effective (and honest) than "When you yell at me, you turn into a crude, ugly, aggressive boor."

4. Finally, fight for understanding, rather than to score points or to prove the other person wrong.

You see, if one person loses, you both lose.

What that means in practice is be curious. Use conflict as a way to discover what is happening under the surface, between you two.

The special thing about fighting for the sake of understanding is that it implies commitment. It says, "I love you enough to struggle with you, rather than just slink away." So it helps your partner feel secure. People who feel safe tend to fight clean and are not afraid to make compromises.

A few years ago, a magazine published my all-time favourite picture of a couple in conflict. It shows a man and woman dressed as boxers in a ring. Apparently at the end of their match, they have big smiles on their faces and are holding their hands up together in the air in victory. What their faces seem to be saying is "We both won. Because we won, I won."

LEARNING AT HOME ABOUT CONFLICT

Every couple is in some ways a "mixed marriage." That is, each of you comes from a background so different from the other's that unless you discuss openly what you learned about marriage from your parents, you will never understand how each other behaves in the new family you've created. Nor will you ever agree on how to handle conflict.

So take some quiet time together, leave the phone off the hook, and agree not to answer the door for an hour. Now, one of you can close your eyes and get comfortable, while the other slowly reads what follows:

"Let me take you back in time now, in your imagination, to childhood. (Pause.) Remember a time when your parents were in conflict with each other. If you can't actually remember an actual incident, it's okay. Just pretend, make one up. It will work just as well. And if you had only one parent or none, you can remember other important figures in your life. (Pause.)

"Now, I'm going to help you remember the scene. What is the place or the room where the conflict is happening like? (Pause.) What are Mom and Dad wearing? (Pause.) Where are you? Who are you closest to physically? (Pause.) Who are you closest to emotionally? (Pause.)

"What is Mom saying? (Pause.) What is Dad saying? (Pause.) And what are you feeling? (Pause.)

"Now take a minute or two to come back to this real room, on this real day. Leave your fantasy behind, open your eyes when you are ready, and be with me." (Pause.)

When you have finished this fantasy, talk together about what the rememberer experienced, and about what you have learned from this about how you handle conflict. How are you like, and unlike, your parents? Have the feelings that you experienced while a child affected the way you handle conflict today?

You may find, as many do, that you tend to behave in ways that your parents did, whether you like those ways or not. Some, however, found their childhood homes sufficiently uncomfortable that they made a conscious or unconscious pact with themselves not to behave as their parents did. These people often turn out to be the polar opposites of their parents. For instance, offspring who habitually sweep trouble under the mat may have had parents who yelled at each other all the time or were physically violent.

Either way, we are always affected in some manner by the powerful emotions in our families. But knowledge is power; knowing these things, the two of you have a lot more choice about what happens, next time you have to deal with conflict.

Once you have talked about these memories, change roles, and have the other person read through the memory trip, with the former reader as the rememberer.

This experience may bring strong emotions to the surface. Don't fear them. Let them flow, and then experience the relief and healing that they bring.

A RULE FOR CONFLICT

Prepare yourselves with a pencil and a sheet of paper for each of you. Sit where you cannot see each other's paper.

Now, write a rule for your partner: "Whenever things are tense between us, I want you to _____." (Fill in the blank.)

Now share your rules with each other. You may get a few surprises, but listen closely. This rule for conflict may turn out in the long run to be a beautiful wedding gift.

CHAPTER SIX

Life in Couples

Everyone wants to be part of a couple. Our spirits insist upon intimacy. Only a few individuals, their emotions somehow deeply damaged, lack this intense need for unity.

Life in couples has a persistent, enduring, quality, often uplifting the people involved, occasionally destroying them. It can survive war and holocaust, career and child-rearing, distance and illness, even, perversely, dislike or active hostility.

Whether heterosexual or homosexual, whether the couple are of similar or different cultural backgrounds, their life together can be accurately described as a "mixed blessing"—at times joyful, at times demanding, requiring and rewarding constant, patient attention.

A WEDDING DOES NOT A MARRIAGE MAKE

What is "marriage"?

Whenever I write here about marriage, I intend the whole realm of all serious, committed love relationships. It includes, of course, all those people who have been wedded in religious or civil ceremonies, but it is not limited to them.

Many a couple has been married without ceremony. Some have wedded themselves together in whispered vows while sitting at breakfast or walking across a bridge some afternoon.

Others never made promises at all, but somehow discovered after many years together that they have been wedded by time and affection.

A formal wedding does not a marriage make. The point is not *how* you join your lives, but *whether*.

When dictionaries define marriage, they include the phrase, "Any intimate union." And that is really the point. If you and your partner happen not to be formally wedded, resist the temptation to skip forward whenever you encounter the word "marriage" in this book.

Don't tell yourself that it applies only to those who have undergone ceremonial nuptials. Instead, hold your relationship, along with what is written here about marriage, up to the light together, and check how well they match each other. If yours is an intimate union, this is all about you.

A "HOPELESS" MARRIAGE COMES TO LIFE

For many months, Trevor maintained he was terribly unhappy in his marriage, and said the situation was hopeless. But the end result of his complaints turned out to be a pleasant surprise for all.

Here is how the relationship looked from Trevor's point of view. First of all, he figured he had made a major mistake in marrying Joan. They were not really suited to each other, he said, and he wasn't at all sure he loved her. And she was starting to catch on to that.

In addition, only a year ago he had an affair which she had recently found out about. So all hell was breaking loose: tears, anger, hurt, jealousy, guilt, the works.

Besides, Joan and his parents didn't get along. And, on top of that, she wanted babies, while he wanted to be free to travel.

Well, with those odds stacked against them, you would think that Trevor and Joan had only a tiny chance of making it as a couple. But then you would be missing the creative power of Trevor's determination.

With his own level of frustration and confusion at an all-time high, it would have been understandable had Trevor simply decided at this point to chuck the whole thing. Instead, he became profoundly curious about the forces that were motivating him, factors that did not necessarily show on the surface of his life.

For instance, he had vaguely sensed for some time that one of his major personal needs was to separate himself more from his parents' influence. For example, he still consulted them about every major decision he made.

Gradually now, over the course of a few months, he turned that insight into action as he began to develop a greater independence. Of course, the unexpected side effect of that was that it provided him with vital space in his life, enough space in fact that he could move closer to Joan and share the decision-making with her.

He also discovered that there was a secret part of him that loved children. He noticed how easily he played with other people's kids, and he wondered whether he might turn out to be a decent father after all.

And after a while, he and Joan started to talk together about the frustrations they both had about their relationship. As a result of these conversations, they made several significant changes, some on purpose, some without realizing what they were doing, in how they operated as a couple.

Now, you can begin to guess where it all stands today.

Not only are Trevor and Joan still together, but they are very much in love. They're looking forward with great eagerness to the arrival of their first baby in a couple of months. Trevor is going to be a dad, and he's sure excited about it.

All of this took determination and a willingness to change, on the part of Joan as well as Trevor. It turned out that the situation wasn't hopeless at all. But, till then, Trevor had never realized how his own distress could help make positive things happen. The result was a victory of hope for him, Joan, and their future child.

KEEPING YOUR RELATIONSHIP ALIVE

A man who came to see me recently was complaining about how hard it was to keep his love affair going. With a straight face, he said, "If you have to work at a relationship, then it's not worth it."

I almost fell out of my chair. He had somehow managed to keep himself ignorant of the most elementary fact about relationships, that we all have to work to keep them healthy.

Once upon a time, it may have been true that people didn't have to pay much attention to their relationships. What held them together, like glue, was sheer survival.

They didn't have to like each other. They had to get the crops into the barn before the rains came, and protect their children from danger.

Nowadays, survival is generally not such a big issue. But the forces which divide couples are multiplying: job pressures, anonymity, affluence, mobility. So today, couples have to work at their relationships to protect them from these destructive forces.

And what does that word "working" mean? It means turning off the distractions, including the television, to take time to talk about us. It means exposing the tensions between us, and not running away from the possibility of conflict. It means going for a walk in the evening without the children, and making love in the afternoons.

Needless to say, the man who told me it's not worth working at relationships, did none of those things. And it took only a few weeks for his relationship to die of starvation. Worse still, I don't suppose he learned a thing from that misadventure.

May your imagination and curiosity about life never fail you as his did.

STAGES OF A MARRIAGE

Marriages sometimes appear to simply stretch out over time like uncut pieces of cloth, but the truth is very different. Almost every long-term marriage goes through five more-or-less predictable stages that might be said to resemble the panels of a tapestry.

These stages are the Honeymoon phase, followed by Procreation, then Turbulence, the Empty Nest, and, at length, Retirement.

While some marriages may skip a stage, and in others the stages may merge imperceptibly into each other, this pattern will fit the experience of most couples.

Reading about these stages will help you take a fresh look at your own life as a couple. And if you understand the predictable aspects of your relationship, you'll have more energy with which you can better tackle the many parts of your life that remain totally unpredictable. You will be encouraged as you see how normal your relationship is for the stage you are at, and that re-assurance will help you summon the courage to tackle whatever threatens the pleasure of growing old together.

Why are there stages in couple life? Because different tasks, like getting to know each other, or having children, are appropriate for a marriage at different times.

The factor that complicates this otherwise straightforward picture is that each individual also has his or her personal life agenda with its own distinct stages. This clash between two individual agendas and the tasks of the couple explains much of the discord in family life today.

Life for a couple today is infinitely more complicated—and therefore more prone to breakdown—than it was for our ancestors. After a very short Honeymoon period, they got right down to Procreation, after which there followed a relatively brief period during which their children looked after them.

All that has changed. Education, affluence, and modern medicine have delayed the the formation of couples by a decade, from puberty to the twenties. They have also provided us with an unprecedented period of independence from children, because we live longer, and this new independence gives us the potential for either extended misery or the most wonderful joy together during the latter years of life.

This time usually begins in our forties; it allows for the development of three new phases. Except for occasional, exceptional couples in the past, these phases constitute a new structural evolution for the human race: the Turbulence phase, the Empty Nest, and Retirement

Each of the five stages has its own particular joys and sorrows. There are challenges which may belong in one stage but will not afflict the others, although the way in which any of them are resolved may deeply influence the years that follow.

Knowledge is power. When a couple suddenly find that they have run into problems in their relationship, it is often reassuring to realize that this is not the end they may have feared, but simply a sign that they have moved to another natural phase.

Knowing that their relationship is "normal," in other words that it is following a path roughly similar to that of others around them, offers two benefits. First, it can make all the difference between despair and peace of mind. In a frantic world, we need all the reassurance we can get. Second, it offers couples a perspective on their lives, a sense of structure and order, which gives them tremendous creative power as, like architects, they design and build their own unique life together.

ONE: THE HONEYMOON

The first stage of marriage is the well-known Honeymoon Phase. Whether it lasts a few weeks or a few years, it is very intense, full of affection and gentle touches. Generally this Honeymoon begins at the time that the pair recognize that they love each other, continues through the process of making decisions about living together, marriage, and so forth, and covers a period of time of varying length thereafter during which they put those decisions into action.

Because the couple's life is relatively uncomplicated at this stage, and their self-awareness is not well-developed, it is easier to keep the romance and intimacy fresh between them than it will be at any other time of their lives.

This is a good thing, because this phase carries with it two major challenges: to get to know each other really well, and to set a style for their life together which will keep the lines of communication open and constantly renew their affection.

The major problem they are likely to run into as they get to know each other, is the inevitable discovery of things about each other which they don't much like.

There is a natural sense of disappointment in discovering that the other person is not Prince or Princess Charming, is not exactly the fantasy person you started out with. But it can also be a joy to discover the unexpected strengths and hidden talents that this person has brought to your relationship.

When it comes to patterns, the danger is that couples may get stuck in ruts of their own creation. For instance, as soon as couples start making complaints that begin with the phrase "You always...," it is an unmistakable sign that they have commenced on a familiar pattern, of expecting the worse—and usually getting what they expect. Unless they deal with it now, this pattern is likely to give rise to love-eroding anger and hopelessness that will last the rest of their life together.

Other destructive patterns which couples may fall into during the Honeymoon include mistrusting each other financially, giving each other only the leftovers of their energy after work and friends have had the cream of it, or fighting chronically without ever resolving their disagreements.

Still, this phase provides the loving basis for all that will follow in the couple's relationship, and at best its beauty and affection will remain available to them throughout the marriage.

TWO: PROCREATION

Next comes the Procreation or Child-Rearing Phase. Now the adults may experience mild disappointment. They have fallen in love, they have conceived children as an expression of that love, but, ironically, they may tend to lose touch with each other, as a result of the natural demands of their young children.

Because it usually occurs at the stage when people are beginning to enjoy the opportunities that their careers offer, this generative stage may produce other "offspring" besides human children, as for some, the parental energy is sublimated into their work. They procreate balance sheets, art, clothing, or medicine.

Struggling to make it up the career ladder, they are often too distracted to devote much attention to family life. The unhappy result is often a deep chasm between the interests of the person who has become the primary parent and the one whose major concern is their vocation.

So at this stage, the marriage tends to be focussed more on children and career than on mutual love.

The challenge here for couples is to make certain that their relationship gets the attention it deserves, if it is to provide a solid foundation for the family as a whole. No couple succeeds perfectly at this, but those who have done best are those who have made a substantial commitment to time shared together in private intimacy.

THREE: TURBULENCE

In their late thirties or forties, couples commonly shift into the Turbulence phase, which corresponds with the "mid-life crisis" in the life of an individual.

In a family where work and child-rearing have been split along traditional lines, the husband may have experienced success at work by now, may have reached many of his lifelong personal goals, and may now be beginning to question whether job success is going to bring him happiness. The wife, meantime, has launched their children into school, so that they no long need her minute-by-minute attention. She may be deeply involved in further education or a career, and she certainly wants to be appreciated for something other than keeping a household running smoothly.

So, to call this stage "turbulent" is putting it mildly. As it supersedes the Procreation phase, it calls into question the priority of procreation that has guided the human race from its earliest days until now, and which in any case has steered the course of most parents' lives until they reach this point.

Now all the couple issues, once obscured by the easy-going haze of the Honeymoon period and by the overwhelming demands of the Procreation Stage, begin, like distant figures emerging from fog, to loom more clearly. There will be no escaping them, as children and career shrink in importance and the inescapability of the couple's dependency on each other grows.

But here too may begin the mellow afterglow, a feature of twentieth-century longevity which in other ages could only be experienced by the occasional, fortunate few.

FOUR: THE EMPTY NEST

The fourth phase of married life is the Empty Nest. This is where the children fly the coop, leaving home to establish their own lives. Couples often change homes at this point, settling more comfortably in a smaller nest, but in the process further disrupting an already fast-changing life.

From this point onward in married life, each stage depends on the last, and, in this case, how the Empty Nest works out will hinge on how well the Turbulence stage was resolved.

At worst, the couple may now resemble two strangers, eyeing each other suspiciously from opposite sides of their empty nest. No chicks remain, to buffer their anxious hostility. They have settled for lives of quiet desperation, substituting need for love.

Yet, at its best, the Empty Nest can provide another, much longer Honeymoon. It sustains a more mature, deeper-running intimacy than the first one, based on a multitude of shared memories and the fulfilling experiences of mutual support.

FIVE: RETIREMENT

The final stage of a marriage is Retirement. As work declines in importance, the couple discover that they have time on their hands, and nothing to distract them from each other. Here new aspects of the personality emerge—or are they noticed for the first time? Here may appear a glittering strength, there a gentle humility. Here too, for the first time, partners may notice other, less endearing qualities.

If the pair still have not resolved their differences, the quiet desperation of the Empty Nest may develop into a desperate, cold bitterness. The fury of such people toward one another can seem frighteningly intense to an outsider, based as it is on their trapped feeling. Both parties have given up all their options for a better life in the name of security.

Retired people who have maintained contact with the therapist aspect of their personalities sometimes come to grips with these problems and make changes which can heal old wounds.

On the other hand, couples who have kept on growing together now discover, despite their manifold differences, a profound and beautiful intimacy. And their physical vulnerability, as their lives approach an end, often leads them to a deeper, even more loving, interdependence.

THE HAPPY COUPLE, AND QUALITY TIME

"We're not as close as we once were. Something has gone out of our relationship."

If this sounds familiar, you may also recognize that scared, panicky feeling that what you have lost cannot be found again. But the happy truth is that this problem is something you can fix.

If you take the trouble to probe this relationship, you will often discover that your unhappiness has a great deal to do with busy lives. All your attention may be going to the job, the children, preparing meals, cleaning the house, and, at long last, sleeping.

Unfortunately, you cannot maintain a happy, lively, relationship as a couple—certainly not in this decade—without regular times when the two of you are alone together. People who try to live without such intimacy are like investors who spend all their capital and then wonder why the bank closes them down. You have to maintain a healthy emotional cashflow.

For couples who want to re-establish communication, one of the most effective techniques is to start planning some high-quality time together. A tiny twenty minutes each day when neither the kids, the phone, the TV, nor the doorbell has priority over your relationship. And by quality time, I don't mean those last sleepy minutes of the day before you conk out.

The key to these times is to talk with one another about your relationship, about your feelings for each other, and about the winds and tides in your own individual lives. You will be amazed at how refreshing even twenty minutes alone together can be.

Such openness to each other is not always easy, but nothing worthwhile ever comes easy, and to say, "Here's how I really feel" can indeed make you extremely vulnerable.

There is always a kind of fearful nakedness in true communication.

But for couples who want to reawaken their passion for each other, and to keep it alive, there is simply no substitute.

THE FEAR OF VULNERABILITY

When Duncan and Colleen first arrived for couple therapy, Duncan seemed to be petrified. A big, strong man, he spent most of the hour looking at his feet. Later, as he became a little more comfortable, he began to talk about what was causing his uneasiness.

Basically, for all his physical power, Duncan felt like an emotional weakling. He was particularly scared of being ganged up on, fearful that the therapist would blame him for all the failures in his relationship.

He said he imagined that Colleen would get a lot of support and he would end up isolated like a criminal.

He was also very anxious about how vulnerable he was in therapy. He felt as though if he said anything, Colleen could use his words to lash back at him.

But what actually happened surprised him.

First of all, the therapist said he was not there to judge him. "Everyone has problems with relationships. So just think of me as a consultant," he suggested.

"Like a company might hire a consultant, you hire me, when you need the well-trained objectivity of a outsider to help you solve your own problems. I'm your employee, not your judge."

Therapy did not turn out to be a gang up on Duncan, because his therapist understood that just as it takes two people to make a relationship, it takes two to wreck it.

It is true that Duncan became more vulnerable in the process. But what did vulnerability mean? It meant being so open, so undefended, that he could easily be hurt by his loved one.

As Duncan thought back to his earlier times of joy with Colleen, he remembered that they were times when they were both unguarded, entirely open to whatever might be said or done. Those periods of vulnerability were among the most creative times in their relationship.

In fact, he realized, the foundations of their love were laid when they were emotionally exposed to each other, when they gave each other the gift of trust.

Sensing that Duncan was making himself vulnerable to her for the first time in many months, Colleen allowed herself to become more vulnerable too.

Now, as if in a dance, they moved back and forth, advancing when they felt courageous and retreating when they were scared, until each gradually allowed the other to touch their very souls.

So they began to heal, and as their relationship became more healthy, the vulnerability Duncan had feared turned out to be the thing that helped save it.

COUPLES TALKING ABOUT FEELINGS

The expression of feelings in a relationship is like having a tank full of gas in a car. The emotions provide an energy and a passion, sometimes an internal explosion, that makes the motor of the relationship turn.

When those feelings are not expressed, the relationship cools off and slows down, till it is parked on the shoulder, going nowhere.

Because no one wants to get stuck, you would think that every couple would check the gauge, make sure they have a full tank, concentrate on their communication above everything else. But the facts are otherwise.

Despite the amazing growth of communications technology in our society—satellites, fibre optics, data processing, and so on—good personal communication is becoming dangerously rare. It almost seems as though the external noise of the information explosion is drowning out the inner voice of intimate relationships.

For most couples it is easy enough to pay attention to facts: "The stock market is up—or down." "There's pizza or steak for supper," "The dog needs a bath," "The baby needs a bottle."

Facts, facts, and more facts.

But somewhere the feelings can get lost.

If you are serious about your relationship, be sure to make time to focus on the feelings that first turned on the ignition. Talk about your love for each other, and about how each other's kindnesses affect you. And don't be afraid to talk about anger, fear, and sadness. Discussing all those important aspects of your life together will keep your emotional fuel tank full and your relationship moving smoothly forward.

"DID I MISS THE HANDWRITING ON THE WALL?"

Fred looked pretty worried. He said he didn't understand what was going on in his marriage, but he was spending very little time with his wife, and he was beginning to think that their relationship was in trouble.

Then he asked, "Are there any clues I should be looking out for?"

The question may seem naive, but Fred was actually well ahead of the game. People are often utterly surprised when their relationships break up. They plunge into a state of shock and confusion, asking, "What didn't I see? Did I miss the handwriting on the wall?"

Fred had already noticed the most important clue: his own absence. It had happened gradually, not intentionally, and he'd hardly noticed. But, no question about it, he was avoiding his wife.

Watch for handwriting on your wall: are you spending most of your energy outside the relationship, whether in alternative relationships or solitary pursuits?

A Yes answer means danger ahead.

Among alternative relationships, the most obvious is a sexual affair. Our society is alert to affairs, intrigued by them, and generally condemns them, but it tends to ignore the fact that people very commonly take less obvious lovers than human beings.

For instance, if you are getting over-involved in a club or association, in religious life, or (the most common of all) in your work, you might argue that it's because you have so much healthy life energy that it spills over into all your activities.

But it should alert you to the possibility of problems in your relationship. For instance, you may be starved for affection and feel you get more warmth from the people elsewhere than you do at home.

You may also be running away from your primary relationship, desperately going anywhere else, to anyone else.

If, on the other hand, your time is going into an activity that actually shields you from relating to people, it can provide a clue to the possibility that in addition to a troubled relationship, you are also dealing with potentially serious depression.

People in this situation include those who watch a lot of TV, video movies, or sports events—or pursue solitary hobbies like computer programming or drinking.

The fact that you enjoy either alternative relationships or solitary pursuits does not, in itself, prove that there is trouble in your marriage. But your preoccupation can function as a challenging reminder to examine how the two of you feel about each other, and to consider giving some therapy to your most precious relationship.

HOW MARLENE'S AFFAIR HELPED HER MARRIAGE

Marlene was in tears, wracked with guilt. Although married, she was in the middle of a passionate sexual affair with another man.

But as she began to explore what her affair meant to her, the things she discovered had much more to do with her marriage than with the other man.

Marlene and her husband had gradually become stuck in a routine, comfortable life. They didn't fight, but they had begun to give their jobs more energy than their marriage. And their sex life was definitely on the skids.

In fact, they had blundered into the perfect set-up for an affair, for even the most complacent human beings have a deep bubbling energy for life and relationships. When couples allow their daily lives to get boring, then unconsciously they start to look around, and to flirt a little.

Without actually intending to bed down, they're fluffing up the pillows.

And then, before they know it, they're "in love."

People commonly say that an affair is the cause of a marriage breakup, but that is often not true. In fact, Marlene's affair was a symptom of trouble, not the cause. And the cure, which was not at all easy for her, required that she put her energy back into her marriage, and start working on it.

This may sound a little perverse, but there is a good chance that Marlene's affair actually saved her marriage.

UNPREDICTABLE RESULTS OF A SEXUAL AFFAIR

You could see why Mary ended up having an affair. Her husband Cam was weak, and their relationship was a bore. Once the affair was over, she came right back to him. And boy, did she get a surprise!

Cam could never say no to Mary. True, he was pretty hurt when he found out about her love affair, but he accepted it. Even when she moved in with the guy, he didn't raise much of a fuss. Or anything else.

He didn't date, he just stayed home, where he watched TV and he read some books about psychology. And whenever Mary felt a little insecure in her affair, there he was, waiting for her.

Good old Cam the doormat.

Well, one day Mary got dumped. End of the affair. Within an hour she was on the phone to Cam. But to her amazement, Cam in his quiet and hesitant way, told her no.

No, he wasn't prepared to pick up where they'd left off. And no, he didn't know if he'd ever trust her again. Slowly but surely, Cam was growing healthier and more assertive.

So it turns out that there is one predictable thing about affairs. They always change the individuals concerned.

And there is one unpredictable thing, which is how they will change.

If you don't like the way your marriage is going, I'd suggest you do some work together on it. Because the alternative, having an affair, is like opening a can with the label torn off. You never know what you'll end up having for supper.

WIFE-BATTERING: AN ADDICTION

Since the dawn of time, men have beaten their wives. It doesn't take a lot of talent. They're bigger and they're stronger, so by and large they get away with it. And, until recently, our society has conspired with them, by putting up a wall of silence around the abuse.

If you are a battered wife, you probably live a very lonely life. Much of the time you're too ashamed to open up about your problems to other people. You may fear that talking might stir up more trouble in your already much-too-risky life. So you hang in, hoping you can help this troubled person you live with, and trying desperately not to provoke him into another assault.

Yet, over the months, nothing much changes, except that you get a little older and more tired, and your children become more frightened.

There is a way out. Specialists have raised the possibility that abuse is an addiction like alcoholism. According to this theory, you may be addicted to his neediness, his lack of control. So your way out is to beat your addiction.

The theory makes some sense. As a female, you were probably raised with certain traditional expectations, one of them being that you should look after other people. And you may still be hanging onto an irrational belief that, if you just find the key to his problems, you can help make this man better. That's why you don't leave.

Yours is an addiction to looking after him, an addiction to helping.

And, of course, he is addicted too, to you. He needs someone to blame when he's upset and angry, and you're handy. He may be scared and intimidated on the streets, but at home he has you for his punching bag.

It is even possible that he is addicted to his guilt.

One thing is certain. You have been living with empty dreams, because you cannot change an addicted adult. Only he can do that, and only if he wants to in his heart of hearts. So stop banging your head against that wall.

If you truly want all this to change, the first step is just like dealing with any other addiction. You have to admit to yourself that you have a problem.

Now, doing so does not excuse the abusive male, but it does get you into motion, making the only changes you can make in this situation. There is no guarantee, but if you stop providing him with a punching bag, he may come to his senses and deal with his problems. But don't hold your breath.

The one sure thing is that gradually you can gain the momentum necessary to escape assault and to break down the wall of silence around your life. And for that, the best and proven strategy is to surround yourself with people who will support you, such as a women's support group, a feminist therapist, or a women's shelter.

Seek them out. It is urgent that you not be alone, as you begin to break the grip of these two interlocking addictions.

BECOMING VULNERABLE

Leonard and Lisa are a couple so independent of each other that, at first sight, they appear extremely mature.

But when you get to know them, it becomes sadly clear that they are like frightened little children, constantly keeping each other at a distance, and so avoiding the risk of becoming vulnerable to each other.

Self-sufficiency is not always what people assume. Rather than being a mark of maturity, for some it functions as a safety net intended to soften their landing should their partner either fail to catch them or let them down. An independence founded on fear, it makes what they most desire from their relationship, intimacy, next to impossible.

These two young professionals have been married for three years, and they are beginning to recognize that a part of their relationship has failed to gel. In their frankest moments, they now admit that living with each other is almost like living with a room-mate. They respect and like each other, but there is no passion now, and they rarely make love.

Part of the problem is the way it all started. When Leonard and Lisa met, they were in their late twenties and already established in separate careers. When they moved in to an apartment together, feeling somewhat tentative and understandably cautious about over-committing themselves, they maintained their own separate friendships, separate sports activities, and—of course—separate bank accounts.

When they formally married a year later, nothing changed.

They never let themselves become a single unit, a couple. Or as that scandalous old phrase has it: "One flesh." They have remained very much two separate, secretly scared, individuals.

It would be no help at all to them to return to the solutions of the good old days, in which one of the partners, usually the woman, submerged herself in the other's identity. That done, the roles were clear and the uncertainty minimal. But the cost was high. Being submerged is just a breath away from drowning.

The woman had to assume a childlike role along with the demands of being a wife and parent. Margaret would never willingly trade her hard-won self-sufficiency for that.

No, the point is that they both, man and woman, need to face their fear of being overwhelmed by the power of the other. Leonard and Lisa will have to take some risks before their relationship will gel, risks that will symbolize a new openness.

It hardly matters exactly what they do—telling each other their secret thoughts, spending time with each others' friends, playing squash together, combining their bank accounts, or something else. What is important for them, and for many of today's couples, is to change the style of their lives, so that they reflect their commitment to each other.

As they face their fears, they will gradually grow into a mature couple.

GAYS STRUGGLE FOR FAMILY LIFE

Many cynics believe that homosexuals became interested in commitment only after the AIDS epidemic made promiscuity mortally dangerous. Others follow the popular prejudices, that lesbians and gay men are more interested in a good time than in long-term relationships.

These myths are far from true. In fact, many homosexuals long for a solid family life, and many have already found it.

Then why do the myths abound? Because our society is so cruel to homosexuals, most of them, for their own protection, tend to live inconspicuously, in the shadows. Straight people don't know them—or don't know that they know them. As a result, our information is faulty.

Understandably, the media only tell us about the criminals and the crazies—who are also well-represented among heterosexuals. We are much less likely to read about the fidelity of gays and lesbians in their relationships, or about their many acts of sacrificial love.

Another problem is that while they may love each other as much as straight people do, there is no legal recognition, much less support, for their relationships. Like an increasing number of straight people, gay couples have learned to rely on their commitment rather than on the formality of a marriage licence. But the drawback is that as a society we rarely support them, and as a community we rarely celebrate their love.

To their credit, gays have responded by developing commitment ceremonies which are like weddings, so that friends and family can gather round and express their backing for their union. That not only promotes but authenticates good relationships.

It also reminds us that, apart from their being attracted to their own sex and being discriminated against as a result, the emotional qualities of homosexuals are just like those of heterosexuals.

Gay people are simply people. Their hearts hunger for love and emotional security. And, just like straight folk, when our relationships get a little rocky, they need good friends around to counsel and encourage them.

WOMEN'S POWER IN THE LIFE OF A COUPLE

A major problem that couple relationships face is the power that men have traditionally exercised over women. The uneven distribution of authority has diminished the entire family's vitality, and proven unsatisfactory for all family members, including those supposedly powerful males.

Males have kept females out of politics, controlled the family purse strings, and, in too many tragic cases, emotionally bruised and physically broken their women.

Where they got away with it, they have been supported by the entire apparatus of a patriarchal society, and, unhappily, by the women themselves, many of whom have been very passive. In fact, in most societies throughout most of recorded history, women have been conditioned to see themselves as victims.

But in this age women are hearing a countervailing message: it is time for you to discover your strength as a female, for, as long as you allow a man to control your life, neither of you will be happy.

Now, to a woman who is terrified because of physical beatings, that may be little comfort. The best advice for her is to find a women's hostel, get support, get out, and stay away from the man who is abusing her.

But in cases that do not involve actual abuse, when a woman demands equal power with her man, there are usually two predictable and ultimately positive results.

The first is that the man often turns a little sulky for a while. He may be angry and upset by the turnabout. That is not admirable in itself, but it is understandable, because he is readjusting his expectations of the most important relationship in his life. He will get over it.

This is a natural phenomenon, so don't let it panic you.

The second result is that, being conditioned from childhood to admire strength, the man will find that he really likes it in either sex. His new respect for his partner will actually strengthen the bond between them.

Wise farmers have always known that when two horses are harnessed together to haul a heavily-loaded wagon, the job is accomplished best when their power is evenly matched.

It is no less true that the very best marital team to meet today's challenges consists of a powerful man pulling side by side with a powerful woman.

LEARNING ABOUT CONFLICT FROM INDUSTRY

When people are all steamed up and conflict is in the air, it can be pretty upsetting for everyone. Most people are frightened by confrontations. They worry that this blowup could mean the end of a relationship, or even of a career.

But conflict can be wonderful, and well-managed conflict is amazingly creative, a real gold mine for families, businesses, and organizations that seek excellence in all they do.

Success depends on solving problems. What conflict does is to force us to look at problems from new and different points of view: mine, yours and theirs.

At work, even if we don't like a colleague, his or her perspective may stimulate our own creativity. We develop solutions that we would never have dreamed of if we had avoided the conflict and simply accepted each other's newly hatched (and perhaps half-baked) ideas. A lot of good creative research in science and other areas has resulted from conflicts faced head-on.

So conflict is rewarding. It actually makes our lives more interesting.

As it happens, there are lots of workplaces—and homes, for that matter—where most of the personnel operate in a depressed manner, at about half their capacity. Those are generally places where conflict has been suppressed, and creativity with it.

On the other hand, the most profitable and successful organizations tend not to fear but to encourage conflict. These companies and families believe in their people. They trust human nature, and they have discovered that with most human beings, conflict energizes people, gets their blood flowing and their brains working.

CONFLICT LEADING TO RELATIONSHIPS

Because it stimulates creativity, conflict can be good for business, but the good news is that it can also make your non-professional relationships more successful, whether they are at work or at home.

Much as it may frighten and unsettle us, conflict can actually improve the way people feel about each other.

First of all, conflict provides useful information. Like a big red light that you can't ignore, it says, "Stop. Something isn't going right in this relationship, and we need to deal with that." The emotions that go with conflict remind us that we have choices, either to keep going on the same old hurtful way or to stop and make some changes.

Change is the very lifeblood of healthy human beings, and one of truly great facts about conflict is that it stimulates us to change.

The second good thing about conflict is that when we face our disagreements, we let off steam. Day-to-day irritants tend to collect in any relationship, but when we discharge them, we feel better about each other.

However, the most intriguing fact about conflict is that it increases our knowledge of ourselves. As we reflect on our own emotional reactions, we are bound to discover more about what we like and dislike, and especially about how we let other people push our buttons. That knowledge can help us develop friendships and family ties that leave us strengthened and refreshed.

This concept of conflict may seem like an idealistic dream. Real conflict, some say, is dirty, mean, and hurtful.

This is often true, of course. And that is why it is important to become a therapist to yourself, your home, and your work. As you learn to manage your conflicts more effectively, they can deepen rather than damage your relationships.

DEALING WITH CONFLICT MORE EFFECTIVELY

The problem is not that couples fight, but that they don't know how to fight effectively. Often they're like boxers caught in a clinch—sweating and groaning, shoving at each other and getting nowhere. They're unable to escape, but also unable to look the other in the eye.

But, as 90-Second Therapists, they have the opportunity to break the clinch, pull apart and look at what they're doing wrong. They can become referees in their own match.

It is one of those mysterious paradoxes of life, that whatever you call these angry encounters—fights, conflicts, arguments, scenes, battles, wars, explosions, blowups, or something else— they are actually essential to keeping the peace.

Every couple has things to fight about. So the best way to get along well is to learn how to do it effectively.

As self-referees, there are three bad fight habits you can correct by yourselves that will otherwise keep you from winning together.

The first is making assumptions about each other. For instance, one partner may say, "I'm angry at you." And the other may imagine that means, "You're a bad person."

Instead of checking out the assumption, the "injured" party often imagines that he or will lose the match, unless the other person can be proven wrong. Such people tend to turn either sulky and defensive or aggressively abusive.

Assumption is truly the mother of all screw-ups.

The solution is simply to ask one or two naive questions, as in this dialogue:

"Are you saying I'm a bad person?"

"No, I'm just mad because you didn't keep your promise."

"So you think I never keep my promises?"

"No, I don't think you never keep your promises. I'm just upset about this one, today."

"Oh, I see. Well, maybe you're right...I'm sorry."

Another assumption that often trips people up is the not-surprising misconception that the fight is really about what it appears to be about. For instance, if you imagine that the two of you are fighting about how the toothpaste tube ought to be squeezed, could it be that you are actually upset about not being respected by your partner, or about some other, more significant concern? Let yourself cool down, give it a little thought, and then deal with whatever you discover.

Next to making assumptions, a leading bad habit of couples in conflict is not really listening to each other. They may give the impression that they are paying attention, but the fact is, they are just waiting for the other person to stop for breath, so they can get their arguments in.

Since most people fight in order to be heard, and not simply because they like the noise, this is a terribly frustrating pattern. But the solution is equally simple.

Try phrases such as the following: "Am I getting your meaning right?" "Is this what you want me to hear?" "How come I keep hearing criticism when you say you don't intend it?" "What would you like us to do about it?" "Are you hearing what I'm saying?" "What exactly are you hearing?"

The third bad habit is for couples to throw everything into every battle, including the kitchen sink. An argument about finances leads to harsh words about careers, relatives, the children, or the dog. Faced with such a barrage, no wonder couples feel entirely overwhelmed.

And no wonder they are tempted to fight dirty. Anything to get out from under the barrage that includes even the kitchen sink!

The solution lies in simple, direct statements: "Hey, it's not fair to drag my relatives into an argument about our holidays." "Why don't we stick with the topic." "I know it was me who raised the career issue, but that got us off topic. So let's get back to what we're really fighting about."

Kitchen sink arguments often result from hoarding. People who clear the air regularly are not nearly so tempted to drag in extraneous arguments.

Conflict is normal, and relationships that avoid conflict are ultimately doomed to take a fall. Not to fight is not to be healthy. So the only real question is whether couples teach themselves to fight fairly and effectively.

For couples, unlike boxers, if one of them loses, they both lose. Conflict succeeds in families only when both parties win.

THE ANGRY ART OF HOARDING

There are pros and cons to hoarding. People who hoard are people who value the past. They may still have so-and-so's baby shoes, even the newspaper that first announced her birth. For the right person, this "junk" collection could turn out to be a cherished treasure.

The down side of hoarding is that these people tend to live in the past, constantly mulling over old times and fighting old battles. Rather than move into the future, trusting in their own reserve of abilities, they collect every trinket which might conceivably prop up their fragile lives in a fear-ridden tomorrow.

This is no question about the destructiveness of hoarding in relationships. Whenever two people care about each other, problems are inevitable. Some deal with them and then sensibly discard them, like worn-out shoes, while others hang on and on.

You've probably heard people say with a grimace about their spouses, "He (or she) never forgets." It's pretty obvious that this is not a discussion about remembering appointments. It's about hoarding anger.

Hoarders, as soon as their partners make a mistake, are reminded of the stockpile of hurts they have collected over the years. And whether or not they fight explicitly about those hurts, the venom that accompanies their conflicts clearly has their source in them.

If you are a hoarder, and want to stop, here are the two essential rules:

First, deal with problems when they occur, so that you can let them go. No matter how frightening it may be to confront your friend or partner, it's better than saving up this poison for the next 30 years.

Second, if you two are in conflict, make sure you keep in touch with what is happening in your emotions. You probably have a right to be angry about whatever it was that started the fight.

But if you're feeling out-of-control now, suspect hoarding. Hang onto the real topic of conflict like a terrier hanging onto a bone, but don't attack your spouse for things you should have dealt with long ago.

Maybe you need a good friend to talk to about your memories, someone who will help you give them a decent burial.

WIN/LOSE OR WIN/WIN

Whenever you're in conflict with someone, there is one factor that can make the difference between damaging your relationship and deepening it. That factor is attitude.

For many people, conflict seems destructive and frightening. And that's because they take the attitude that conflict is a win/lose proposition. "I've got to win and you've got to lose," or, "I'm right and you're wrong."

Of course, if it is a question of winners and losers, then they do have to fight hard, and dirty, to make sure they're not the one who loses.

But the win/lose scenario is seriously out of date, whether for couples or organizations. It is a holdover from our simplistic childhood notions, from the days when the bad guys wore black hats and good guys wore white.

There is often an audible sigh of relief when people recognize that the best solution to conflict, at work or at home, is to make it a win/win exercise.

That is very practical advice, because if I know that I'm going to be a winner, then I can afford to be generous, to let you make your points, and to learn from them. That way we both gain.

This is the route to consensus, a rare and beautiful commodity in a competition-oriented world.

None of this is intended to suggest that conflict will never be upsetting, that you will never lose your temper, never suffer criticism. The finest people are fallible, so even in the best relationships these things happen from time to time; however, they are rarely terminal.

Not surprisingly, people who take a win/win attitude to conflict consistently turn out to be...winners.

MY FAULT OR YOUR FAULT?

When conflict raises its ugly head, we are usually tempted to blame the other person. It's your fault, not mine, we think. But the truth is usually not that one person is wrong and the other right, but that we have a shared problem.

I hadn't seen Mike and Doris for therapy since their holiday, and as soon as they walked in, Doris started to shove handfuls of vacation photographs at me. Now, the odd thing was that Mike, who usually made good contact with me, just sat there, looking gloomy and hardly saying a word.

After a few moments of silently asking myself what was going on, I realized I had better raise the question with them. What I found out was that Mike and Doris were in total disagreement about whether to show me their holiday pictures. But they had not dealt with the conflict.

As soon as I raised that issue, Mike said he felt like he was being accused of something, and he backed off even further. It turned out that he had told Doris earlier that he did not want to waste an hour of therapy looking at holiday photographs. But now, in retrospect, he figured that any jury would judge him to be the bad guy—the gloomy, stingy, husband.

On the other hand, I discovered that Doris had her own secret reasons for showing me the pictures. To her, it seemed much safer to keep me entertained for a few minutes at the beginning of the session than to get directly into our therapy work, which, of course, consisted of facing the difficulties in their marriage.

So, despite their fears, it turned out that neither of them was entirely right or entirely wrong about the photos. As usual.

I thought about that, off and on, throughout the session, and, before they left, I suggested a simple phrase to Mike and Doris which will help them face conflict better in the future without either of them having to feel guilty. Here it is, because you can use it too:

"We have a problem."

Note: the phrase is not, "It's your fault," nor, "It's my fault." This magical phrase is, "We have a problem."

So let's talk about it.

TAKING YOUR EXPECTATIONS ON VACATION

Last year Sherry and Elliot took a long-awaited vacation together. A full week alone in the sunny south: exotic food, hot white sand, relaxation, no pressure. And, by the time they got home, they were so angry at each other they could hardly speak.

What happened to them is that they went on vacation with totally different expectations. Sure, they had talked about it, sort of. They knew they both wanted a warm climate, away from their responsibilities for kids and work. But that only touched the surface.

You see, Elliot's unspoken dream was to lie in the sunshine with a good book, in a silence broken only by the cry of the seagulls and the roar of the waves. On her part Sherry had been waiting for months for a chance really to talk with Elliot, to communicate without interruptions from his job, the phone, the TV, or the children.

Well, neither of them got what they wanted. Elliot tried to read, but Sherry kept bugging him to talk. Sherry became entirely frustrated by his isolation, and soon they were both angry. Even then, they didn't talk about it; just sulked some, drank a little too much, and flirted with other people.

What a shame. Had they managed to tell each other ahead of time what they were actually hoping for, they would have found that there was lots of space in their holiday for both to be satisfied. They might, for instance, have spent the mornings walking along the seashore and talking, and their afternoons reading their books.

The moral of the story is not hard to find: before you plan your next vacation, be sure you and your partner discuss in depth how you want to spend it. Make sure you understand each other's hopes. That way, you will both enjoy it so much more.

DEPENDENCY AND LACK OF COURAGE

Everyone knows couples who no longer love each other and simply co-exist, leading lives of quiet desperation that are terminated only at last by death. There have always been marriages like that, couples who feel that they have to stay together because of vows once made or for the sake of children.

But there are also many unhappy couples who feel just as trapped, even though they have no children to hold them together, and, in fact, may not be married but simply living together.

Have you ever wondered what it is that imprisons people in relationships which make them so miserable? There are two major answers: dependency, and a lack of courage.

Obvious examples of dependency are the man who can't cook his own meals, and the woman who doesn't know how to manage the family's money. They both depend on their spouses, not because of love, but because of feelings of inadequacy.

But dependency is frequently more subtle still, and much more damaging. As young children, we were entirely dependent upon our parents, whether they were warm, supportive human beings or cold and abusive. And although we are now adults, who can choose whomever we want to associate with, some of us still cling, in a continuation of that childlike pattern, to people who hurt us and damage our self-esteem.

If a spouse turns out to be that kind of person, the relationship often hits a dead end, with neither partner able to see the way out.

Then there's lack of courage. There are quite a few people around who do not have the guts to get out of bad relationships and start afresh. More common are those who are just not brave enough to confront their partners from within the relationship, and to ask for the kinds of changes that might make it viable.

Yet I often see that when people muster the courage to demand those changes, even apparently hopeless relationships can come back to life.

A COMMITMENT TO COMMUNICATE

The old lady lies alone in a nursing home, her mind scarcely functioning, barely able to keep track of herself, her family, or her friends. Her husband died a long time ago, and soon she will follow him. Yet her journals, written a decade or so ago, when her mind was still fresh and alive, convey some of the wisdom that made her marriage a joy.

One entry reads, "When we were first married, we promised one another that anytime we did not agree we'd never lose communication with one another—we would be free to express how we felt, whether we agreed or not."

They married on November 23, 1929. Then, there were few of the sophisticated supports for relationships which we enjoy today. Little in the way of books or therapists. Yet she and her husband shared a wisdom that was timeless.

Poised over her journal, looking back over their marriage, she measured the results of their commitment to keeping the lines of communication open: "All through the years, we never lost our love and respect for each other."

And her daughter, having discovered the journal while digging through family keepsakes, remembers the quality of her parents' life together and concludes, "What she wrote was true. It wasn't just said. It really happened."

CHAPTER SEVEN

Family Life and Parenting

In family life, we entrust ourselves to each other, highly vulnerable to hurt, often needy, and always growing. To be parents is a sacred trust, increasingly hard to live up to in this complex world. We strive with all our energy to be faithful to the task and to each other, sometimes failing, sometimes stumbling into wisdom.

Family life is not an option but an inescapable reality in our lives. Even the most solitary individuals carry their families around in their heads. Whether as memories or as day-to-day presences, our families whisper powerful, half-noticed messages that can enhance or erode our self-esteem, our confidence, and our joys.

The family, then, is the crucible in which the individual is formed.

NON-DEMAND TOUCH

When I was asked to speak recently at a school for massage therapists, one of the delightful things I noticed was how easily the students touched each other. Casually they would rub each other's shoulder muscles, and from time to time someone would lay a gentle hand on someone else's arm.

Generally, we are a society with a lot of fears about touch. Crowded by our cities, in public transit, elevators, and stores, we try to preserve some physical separateness. And since, occasionally we are harassed by sexual thrill seekers, we tend to suspect every accidental contact.

And yet touch is one of our most basic needs. We know that infants who are stroked or picked up make better progress than those who lie alone in incubators. And we adults are not much different.

The varieties of touch within the family are numerous:

Two hands clasping each other.

Fingers stroking your hair.

A firm hand on your shoulder, your back, or your arm.

A cheek softly grazing your cheek.

The two of you standing shoulder to shoulder, or sitting side by side.

A warm hug.

A cool hand on a sick forehead.

A helping hand across the street.

A gentle kiss of hello, goodbye, or goodnight.

This is non-demand touch, touch that gives for the sake of the other, and asks for nothing in return. It is the special gift of family life.

And how does it work its miracle? That much is simple. It reassures the most primitive part of our being, the infant within, that all is well and that we are loved.

THE HARD WORK OF COMING HOME FROM WORK

Late afternoon can be one of the most stressful times of the day. That is when we make the very difficult transition between the performance-oriented demands of work and the more subtle requirements of family life.

Many people handle this stress, when they get home, by creating a distance between themselves and others, either by being grumpy or by putting up an actual physical barrier such as hiding behind the newspaper. Others avoid the problem entirely, by staying at work until late at night.

But there are many satisfying ways to make this reentry time work better for you, to reestablish contact with your loved ones, and so to gain fresh energy and pleasure.

Here is an easy, practical example. On your way home from work, you can gradually shift the focus of your mind away from the office or factory, and let yourself begin to think about each member of your family. Let yourself become curious about how their day has been, and by the time you arrive home, it will be easier to show them that you're interested.

They'll like that. And they'll love you for your attention to them.

By the same token, if you've been home all day, waiting for your mate to return, you might let yourself imagine how he or she will feel reentering the home. A warm, undemanding greeting can help an over-stressed, traffic-jammed, peopled-out spouse begin to feel human again.

Remember, everyone has some difficulty with the late afternoon transition. That's normal. And it's okay to tell your loved ones that it "feels a little stressful coming home today." By the time you have said that much out loud, you are likely to be feeling better already.

WHERE WILL YOUR CHILDREN WALK?

Despite the unquestionable joys of parenthood, it can be very hard to watch your children grow up. As babies, they are all potential, and, in a single breath, parents can imagine out loud that they will be artists and scientists and athletes, all at once.

But with every year the children's options narrow, as their bodies and minds develop in their own peculiar ways. As a parent, you may find yourself imagining less and wondering more, as you watch them drift at times, then take charge of themselves, drift again, make choices, and shoulder more and more responsibility for their futures, even though they are still children—age 14 going on 34.

So with every year, the stakes get higher. When your one-year-old tries to take those first steps, you bite your lips. But you know that, if not this week, then next week, he or she will walk.

By the time the kids are teenagers, you can no longer predict—or control—where they will walk.

There are hard times raising babies. Dragging yourself out of bed in the middle of the night, you often wonder when you will shake this constant fatigue.

But when the kids grow up a little, you face a different, more subtle exhaustion, as you search for that elusive balance between imposing your hopes on your children and allowing them to develop in their own unique directions.

KEEPING A CARING DISTANCE FROM YOUR TEEN

Parents who were superb at raising little children may make the worst parents for teenagers. That notion comes from Salvador Minuchin, a world authority on the family, and here is why what he says may be true.

The ideal parents of young children are highly involved with the children. They are actually with them a great deal of the time, constantly encouraging and stimulating them. Even when the kids are out of sight, these parents never lose track of the fears or potential dangers their babies may run into.

True, they allow them to take a few independent steps, but that independence is in part an illusion. In fact, there is always an adult just a step behind, waiting to pick them up and comfort them when they fall.

On the other hand, the ideal parents of teenagers are entirely different. Knowing that it is important not to keep the adolescent an infant, they allow many freedoms.

The child may wear clothing that appears outlandish, but the parents hold back from interfering, and in the process discover that they do not have to know every detail of what happens in their teenager's life. In other words, increasingly the child is encouraged to cope alone with the challenges and dangers of life.

That is not to say that ideal parents are uncaring or uninvolved. They are still there for their child, and always will be, until the day they die. But now their challenge is to keep a close eye on the essentials, from a caring distance. That is why there is no stage of parenthood more difficult than when the children are adolescents.

Learning to maintain the delicate balance between parental support and independence is recognized as a major developmental task for adolescents. Well, it is just as urgent for the development of the adolescent's parents, as they learn to let go of their child.

FRESH IDEAS ON CHILDREN AND DISCIPLINE

Parents are often distressed when their partners don't support them on matters of discipline. They play out the old routine called "The right hand doesn't know what the left hand is doing." That game is not good for the kids, and it frequently sets the parents against each other.

For instance, Mom will ask the child to return to the house by a certain hour at night, while Dad very obviously says nothing at all. Or Dad will say, "No more candy today," and Mom will quietly add, "I suppose just one more piece wouldn't hurt."

I say it does hurt. On the surface, the children may think it is great fun to manipulate their parents. But underneath, they wish their parents would be parents, and give them a sense of security, so that they can be simply children growing up.

Parents cannot be expected to agree on everything, but it is important that they make time to decide together where they stand on major disciplinary issues—homework, bedtimes, and household chores—and agree to uphold each other. That done, parents need to talk to the children about their decisions, and to make it clear that they intend to support each other.

A particularly helpful way of communicating that message is for parents to make their unity physically obvious. It is a good idea for them to stand side by side and hold each other's hand while they talk to the child.

Why? Because our children are used to ignoring most of the instructions they are bombarded with. That's the only way to survive in a high-information environment, with radio, TV, advertising, teachers, and parents all giving them conflicting messages.

So if you want your message to get across, make sure they can actually see that you mean it. Two hands joined mean, "We're pulling together," a message young people need to hear, and see.

DISCIPLINE AND SEPARATED PARENTING

Separated parenthood is in no way a bed of roses, but it becomes particularly thorny when the parents want the children to understand that they intend to pull together, that when it comes to important issues concerning the children, they will support each other.

One of the major reasons for this difficulty is the obvious fact that they do not always support each other. They live in different homes and probably hold very different views on a number of important issues, views that are likely to grow more dissimilar as the years go on.

Consciously or unconsciously, their kids are aware of all this, and sometimes exploit their parents' division, to their own detriment.

It is crucially urgent, therefore, that children also know that when it comes to the crunch, in issues like health, safety, life decisions, and discipline, their parents love them enough to make tough decisions together.

So how can separated or divorced parents do it? The initial technique for addressing these issues, no matter what your difficulties with your ex-spouse, is to be in touch by telephone or letter and, wherever possible, come to a common understanding.

Keep in mind that the most important factor in these issues is not to win points or to clobber the other parent. It is to make decisions that will safeguard the children's best interests.

This selfless-sounding phrase, "the children's best interests," can actually be quite dangerous. It can provide a convenient cover when what you and your spouse are really trying to do is to refight your old battles. That is why it is always important to reconsider the positions you take with your ex in private, where you can examine your own motives.

The next important step is to make sure the children understand that your decisions are joint decisions. They know that you two can't live together. They may also know that you are not fond of each other. They may even have successfully played one off against the other in the past. But do they know that when it comes to their welfare, the two of you are united?

Drop a phrase like, "Your mom (or dad) and I have been talking, and we have decided...." That can be reassuring good news to children whose world has become a more insecure place as the result of a marital split.

They may not thank you. There may be parts of them that wish they could still play you off against each other. But deep down, they will feel some peace, knowing that their place in each of your hearts it entirely secure and that your decisions are truly motivated by their best interests.

GOOD PARENTING DURING A CRISIS

Mother and her four-year-old are walking hand-in-hand along the downtown street in a pleasant haze of intimacy. Ahead, a woman steps into a store, leaving her husband to wait on the sidewalk. As they near the stranger, Mother notices that her son's shoelace is undone. They talk quietly, voices muffled by the traffic, and she kneels to retie his shoe.

The stranger glances around quickly to see if anyone is nearby, fails to notice Mother and child who are ducked down out of his line of sight, and, as the traffic unexpectedly becomes quiet, allows himself the pleasant relief of a much-needed fart.

This, however, is no average fart, no muted surreptitious squeak. This is a long, loud eruption with a sound like a thousand bricks tumbling from a dumptruck. The eruption occurs, of course, precisely at the ear-level of the two huddled on the sidewalk, and at once the boy, delighted by the event, begins to laugh.

As his face cracks into merriment, Mother steels herself, and undertakes a rapid internal conversation which requires only three microseconds but summarizes an entire parental dilemma. It goes like this:

"Don't laugh. You don't want to encourage him."

"Of course you can laugh. It's very funny."

"What if he laughs next time Granddad does it?

"What if he feels you disapprove of his natural sense of humour? Does he need a stern-faced mother who will keep him stiff and dull?"

"If you laugh, he might do it himself just for effect, next time you have company."

"The point is that you both think this is very funny, and try as you may to avoid it, you are going to share in the intimacy of laughter. You can feel it coming, can't you?"

Whereupon Mother abandons her dilemma by dissolving into a fit of uncontrollable giggles.

To her relief, the traffic noise increases, covering her laughter, the stranger is rejoined by his wife, and at once they stroll off down the street, apparently unawares. Mother can hardly finish tying the shoe, she and her son are so shaken with laughter. At length they rise, catching each other's eyes and exploding again into helpless mirth, they take hands and resume their walk.

Unfortunately, the stranger and wife have stopped to look into the window of another shop. Now Mother and four-year-old are forced to stagger past them, eyes popping, holding their hands over their mouths to stifle the gales of laughter which threaten to incapacitate them.

Three special things have happened in this brief snippet of their relationship. Mother has shown honesty when she was tempted to conceal her feelings. She and her son have acknowledged together something that unites them but which people rarely discuss: those strange and distracting functions of human bodies, And, most important, they have laughed hard together about it all.

THE PAIN THAT PREJUDICE CAUSES

Recently, my wife and I were training a group of mature professional people at the university, when we were suddenly aware that Donna, one of our students, was very upset.

As we explored what was happening, she mentioned that she was a North American native. She had to tell us that, because in fact she appeared to be of Mediterranean origin. It turned out that, during lunch break, some others in the class, also unaware of her race, had been indulging in some cheap, insulting talk about native people.

As soon as Donna said that she had been hurt by their comments, they began to apologize. "I'm sorry," someone told her, "I should have known better. If I'd known you were an Indian, I'd have kept my big mouth shut."

As genuine as that apology was, it missed the point entirely. In their embarrassment, educated professional people were suggesting that it is acceptable to put down other racial groups, as long as they don't hear the remarks. But, as the native student told them in reply, to talk about people behind their backs is no less poisonous than confronting them face to face.

The poison of prejudice destroyed six million human beings during Hitler's holocaust, and in the past decade it has led to genocide attempts against several native populations around the world. Just as easily, it can hurt your next door neighbour's child, or even your own.

As Donna pointed out in her pain, the answer to prejudice is not to watch what we say. It is to examine what we think.

WHERE CHILDREN LEARN TO BE PREJUDICED

One of the most heart-breaking experiences for parents is to see their child come home in tears, sobbing because the other kids have been calling him or her names. "Paki," "homo," "dirty Jew," "wop," "slant-eyed gook"—the list of insults is endless, and so, for the child, is the pain.

Concerned parents should know three important facts about prejudice.

The first is that there are roots of prejudice in all of us. Children show an almost universal, primitive, fear of those who are different from them and their families. That in itself is quite natural and innocent.

The second fact is that this natural fear turns into prejudice only when the child's home life encourages it. I know that there is lots of prejudice out in the school yard, but kids don't learn it there. They learn it from parents who say there is something wrong with a certain racial, religious, or sexual group. It is easy for such parents to make casual remarks about a group's supposedly sharp business practices, or lack of cleanliness, or sexual prowess, or even the smell of their cooking. The adults may not even be aware that their children are listening. But children are always listening, and they first learn to be prejudiced from their parents.

The third interesting fact is that children who are brought up with high self-esteem show few signs of prejudice. Because they feel secure and self-confident, they don't need to put others down. They know that there is lots of room in our world for people of every colour and faith.

HOW CHILDREN DEVELOP SELF-ESTEEM

Children with high self-esteem seem to be happy and successful. They show few signs of prejudice or other anti-social behaviours. But what exactly is this quality we call self-esteem?

Self-esteem is children knowing that they are of great value. You can see it in their physical stance and in their eyes. I'm not talking about the bully or the arrogant child, I'm talking about an inner confidence that no one can take away.

But why does one child seem to believe in herself or himself, while another gives the impression of defeat? Why does one child attract caring, good people, while another attracts bullies and users? A large part of the answer is how the child is treated at home.

Essentially, self-esteem comes from love. Children with a healthy self-image have discovered that it is okay to take risks and make mistakes. Even in failure, they know that mom and dad love them—unconditionally.

You can actually see the love. These kids get touched a lot, gently and without demand.

These are children who have discovered that it is acceptable to have their own opinions. Even if their parents disagree with them, they let their children know that they are respected.

Such children are corrected, but not criticized. And whenever they develop a skill, or discover something new, their parents are first to applaud them. Children with good self-esteem believe in themselves, and they learned to do that from parents who believed in them first.

LOVE AND THE FAMILY

One of the most confusing topics in family life these day is the meaning of the word "love".

People commonly say that they love swimming—and salads. They love their children, they love their country, they love the new neighbour they met at the party, they love their snazzy new underwear, they love their spouses.

So let's take a look at what love really means, in the context of the family. As you read, think about the quality of your relationships with other adults and with your children.

First of all, love is nurturing. Loving adults care about the well-being of the other person, and truly loving people will undergo considerable sacrifice for the sake of the other.

That is why the old marriage vows said, "for better, for worse."

Second, love is commitment. Love is not "for as long as it feels good." That is not love at all; it is self-indulgence. Love is when you value a person so highly that you intend to stand by him or her. Loving adults will work very hard to keep a relationship healthy.

Third, so you won't think that I have gone off the deep end and completely forgotten about passion and excitement and all that good stuff, let me say too that love does have strong feelings. Feelings of warmth and joy and pleasure and, where it is appropriate, feelings of sexual excitement.

That too is love, but don't fool yourself. Those strong, pleasurable feelings in themselves are just that: strong and pleasurable. They are not the same as love unless nurturing and commitment are also prominent. For those two are the special factors that distinguish a truly giving love from all other loves.

SEXUAL ABUSE OF CHILDREN

A psychiatric textbook published only a dozen or so years ago estimated that sexual abuse of children occurred in only one in a million families. We now know that as many as one in every six children is actually sexually abused.

Here are four important facts about sexual assault on children:

First of all, quite simply, it is against the law. And that is because it is extremely dangerous to the child. It has been documented that many adults who were sexually abused as children, now suffer from serious psychological problems, including low self-esteem, a high level of guilt, and, as you would imagine, severe difficulties in their sexual relationships. We have treated many of them at our Centre.

Second, it is largely men who commit these assaults, many of whom were themselves abused as children. Such males need intensive psychotherapy in order to break this pattern. Otherwise it will pass from generation to generation.

Third, far more male children are at risk than one might imagine. Men who assault younger children often show no preference for girls over boys.

Fourth, mothers are potentially the child's best defence against sexual assault. But, in reality, some women manage to keep themselves unaware of abuse, despite all kinds of evidence. That is because they were themselves sexually assaulted in childhood, and it feels too painful for them to face those memories again.

Sexual abuse is a family problem. If you believe it is a problem in your family, I urge you to get professional help immediately.

If you yourself are involved in the abuse of children, you are probably very anxious and upset about your behaviour. You may have sometimes promised yourself that you will stop. But you know too that when the opportunity arises, you tend to do it all over again.

The idea of being your own therapist does not mean that you should try to deal with every issue on your own. There is no need for you to be the Lone Ranger. In fact, now is the time for that therapeutic, healing part of your personality to reach out to someone competent to help you heal yourself.

The stakes are far too high to keep on muddling through on your own.

STREET-PROOFING CHILDREN

Parents are increasingly anxious these days about sexual assault and other violence against their children.

Wise parents make a point of telling their children to avoid adults who try to tempt them into cars, parks, and buildings. They remind them that uniformed people may offer a safe refuge when they need help. They teach their children the danger signals to look out for and the areas to stay away from.

They do all this, recognizing at the same time that more sexual assaults occur within the circle of family and friends than out on the streets.

If the parents are wise about protecting their children, they also try not to terrify them about their minute-by-minute safety. It is a tough juggling act.

But there is one aspect of street-proofing that is less obvious, and it has to do with self-esteem.

We cannot entirely protect our children from dangerous adults. But the kids least likely to be tempted by them are those who know themselves to be loved and valued within their families. In other words, children with high self-esteem.

Such children know that their bodies are not playthings for adults, and are not to be invaded by outsiders. They will literally fight for the right to self-determination.

So how do you build a child's self-esteem? You do it every time you say, "I love you," or "I like this or that about you".

You do it whenever you show your respect for the child's need for distance and self-determination.

And in particular, you build self-esteem every time you touch your child with caring and respect.

Self-esteem is both the key to inner happiness, and the basic foundation for street-proofing your youngster.

CHALLENGE OF THE BLENDED FAMILY

During the past two decades, the shape of the family has changed forever. It was not so long ago that all we knew was the nuclear family: mother, father, and two or three children. Then the nuclear family was joined by the single-parent family, and more recently the blended family has emerged, growing fast and challenging our creative imagination.

Whatever you call it, the "remarriage family," the "step-family," or the "blended family," it all begins when two adults decide to live together and bring together the children from their previous relationships. There it is: instant family. And instant, usually unexpected, problems.

One difficulty for the adults is that they really chose to live with each other, and not with each other's children. Yet they have to get to know these youngsters, with all their individual quirks and idiosyncrasies, understand them, and parent them, and they hope, come to love them.

To add to the problems of the blended family, most adults find it easier to understand and appreciate their own natural children than their stepchildren. When homelife gets a little tense, they may even think they have to protect their child from the stepparent. In these situations, it is not uncommon for the adults to find themselves on opposing sides, divided by their kids. So there's another unwanted layer of stress added to an already complicated new life together.

Further, divorce and the transition to blended family life are painful for the kids, and it is very common for their parents to suffer considerable guilt about this. They wonder, "Have I done my kids more harm than good?"

Finally, our society can offer few roadmaps for this new territory. There is hardly any collected social wisdom about stepparenting. Few stepparents have family or close friends who can serve as models for how to do it; they may know people who have gone through rancorous divorces or who have had to raise kids alone, but it is rare for them to have close-up relationships with other parents who are imaginatively and cooperatively dealing with this complex new style of family. No wonder stepparents are hungry for support.

ROADMAPS FOR THE BLENDED FAMILY

When two adults, whose previous mates have died or, more frequently, have been divorced, bring their children with them into a new home, they are creating a blended family. This is an odd form of relationship, relatively rare, complete with its own problems and its own special solutions.

Being a stepparent is definitely no piece of cake. In the blended family, both parents and kids have to learn to tolerate styles of relating very different from what they are used to. And because the children are often still quietly committed to the previous marriage, they may try to sabotage the new parental team.

Here are four suggestions.

First, appreciate the positives. If you two adults are happier in this new family, then you are creating a happier home for your children to grow up in.

Second, when you're feeling a little frantic, wondering if you are losing your sense of direction, it is important to realize that everyone involved in a blended family finds it a challenge. Give yourselves time to work things out.

Third, you adults need to talk, talk, and talk some more, about your new family and about your own feelings. Make sure you let down your defences, so you don't waste the opportunity by trying to justify yourself or your kids. Learn to talk very honestly, and really train yourself to listen.

Finally, you need some roadmaps. Seek out and cultivate friends who themselves have experienced a blended family. Join a stepparents' group, ask others to introduce you to people who have blended families.

After all, you are pioneering in territory that is new to you. It makes no sense to go without maps when you can find support and guidance for yourselves and your kids in your own community.

THE BLENDED FAMILY: A CHILD'S PERSPECTIVE

Children who become part of a blended family usually enter this new life with a strike against them. They may not be as resilient or easy-going as other youngsters, because they are under massive stress as a result of a marriage breakup or, in some cases, bereavement.

If their parent died, they have suffered a loss that no one can make up to them. Grief may take much of their childhood to work through, and in the meantime they may resent anyone who attempts to fill their lost parent's shoes.

In the case of a marriage falling apart, they may have lived through years of strife, then the agony of watching Mom and Dad split up, and at length a bottomless sense of loss. The marriage which was the absolute foundation of their daily life has died.

Now, just as they are getting used to living with Dad or Mom alone, there is somebody new on the horizon, someone who is competing with them for their parent's attention.

In what may seem like no time at all, that new person is living in the same house with them, parenting them, setting them chores, and making rules. Sometimes that person has brought children too, whom they may or may not like. And they, the children, are powerless to do anything about all this because, whether they like it or not, they've got it: a blended family.

The number of children in blended families is increasing by the thousands each year. Once their grief begins to resolve, most of them cope marvellously. They see the stepparent as a person who enhances their life with care and ultimately love rather than as a replacement for an absent mother or father.

In cases where the absent parent was alcoholic, erratic, or dangerous, the new stepparent may come as a great relief. And for an "only child," it can be a dream-come-true to share a home with sisters and brothers.

FAIRY TALES: SELF HELP FOR CHILDREN

Every year hundreds of authors write self-help books like this one, and some of them sell very well. But one of the most intriguing types of self-help literature was written centuries ago primarily for popular entertainment. I mean the "fairy tale."

Not all parents enjoy reading fairy tales to their children. Some fear that they are too violent, while others find them too old-fashioned. I think fairy tales are just right.

What I like about fairy tales is that they help children come to grips with their own inner world. And they do it in a safe and reassuring way, which promises that everything will work out fine in the end.

Here's an example. *Hansel and Gretel* is about children lost in the woods. And in fact the emotional life of a child is very much like a dense forest, dark, and beautiful, and full of danger. There are wild animals within us, and always the fear of an evil witch lurking. So the child often feels lost. But, as the famous child psychologist Bruno Bettelheim once told me, the reassuring truth is that the child who perseveres will escape the forest and ultimately be secure.

Or take *Snow White*. When she is rescued from the wicked witch by friendly dwarves, she discovers that she must keep house for them. Now that may sound sexist, but for both boys and girls, it carries a deep symbolic truth: only through hard work, hard emotional work, will children develop successful relationships with their families and the whole community of their loved ones.

As you can see, these stories bring meaning and hope to the turning points of our lives. As a matter of fact, they have as much to say to adults as to children.

Maybe you'd like to get the Brothers Grimm down from the shelf and read a fairy tale to your partner tonight. Chances are you'll find it speaking to both of you.

POWER AND FAMILY LIFE

Many families today struggle with the proper use of power.

It used to be, in previous centuries, that men held most of the power, and our society continued to support this arrangement long after it had proved itself ludicrous.

To this day, there are men who bully their families, drink too much, or become helpless wimps, because holding all the power is too great a responsibility for anyone. Lord Acton wrote wisely, a century ago, "Power tends to corrupt and absolute power corrupts absolutely."

As a result of the difficulties that males have had with power, women have demanded equality. Their insistence on a share of the power is evident in every age and culture and in the modern Western world, it has emerged through the suffragette and women's liberation movements.

So in many families the power has fallen to women. And because they were naturals, better trained from childhood in the management of relationships and the emotions, they have often taken over.

But to their chagrin, women have not realized all the benefits they had hoped for. Often they have seen their sons shrink from their power, and their husbands fall in love with their jobs, until the males of their households had become passive outsiders at the dinner table.

Most recently, children have begun to fill the power vacuum. As infants in a consumer society, they discovered that a tiny tantrum could get them candy on demand. Now, as teenagers, many have gained the power to smoke or drink or pop whatever they desire, and then to come home late to find that Mom or Dad has kindly turned down the bedsheets.

But in the pain and confusion of a life without adequate direction, they too have discovered that holding all the power in the family doesn't bring happiness.

Now, in case your household is struggling with power issues in the midst of all this confusion, here is the principle of healthy power: it is the recognition that every family member, of every age, has a legitimate right to exercise certain powers. Precisely what those powers should be depends on the varying individuals and family groups involved, a complicated equation to figure out at the easiest of times.

But this much can be said with certainty: all members of your family should feel that they have the ability to make key decisions about their own lives.

Depending on the people involved, these might range from an infant's right to be comforted when frightened in the dark to a young child's right to wear green socks with blue pants, from a teenager's right to decide when to do homework to an adult's right to an hour of peace and quiet on Sunday afternoon.

It is worth asking the members of your family whether they feel they can exercise their legitimate powers. You may get some interesting surprises.

How do you tell whether children who can't yet talk have enough power? The babies are usually doing fine if they wipe their sticky hands on your best sweater while offering you a lopsided grin. Back to the laundry hamper.

A major source of self-esteem, in children and adults, is the respectful and kindly sharing of family power.

HOMEWORK: BREAKING THE POWER BLOCKADE

Some parents find themselves in a constant battle with their children over homework, while the children increasingly see their parents as nags and oppressors. It is very easy to get caught in such power struggles, but loving and effective parents can take quite a different approach.

Instead of trying to force their will on the children, they learn to let the children make their own decisions. The older the child, the more the adults step back.

So, for instance, if their children have been having problems about homework, a parent might say something like this: "I believe you should do your homework every night, but I'm tired of standing over you, trying to make you do it. That's been a mistake. After all, I've already passed grade six. So I intend to let you decide when you'll do your homework. Of course, if you don't do it, you will have to deal with whatever consequences come your way at school. But if you do well, you will know that you deserve all the credit."

Many parents find that a pretty scary idea, easier to talk about than to do. And it is true that at first the children may not get their homework finished. They may even get lower grades for a while.

If handing appropriate responsibility to your child appears not to be working, talk with other parents whose judgment you trust. They may help you see the problem from another angle, perhaps discover that you are inadvertently shooting down your own chances of success.

Whatever happens on the homework issue or on other fronts, for many families there is a more fundamentally important issue involved, which is that the children are given a chance to develop their natural talent for handling responsibility. While that is happening, the parents have a chance to enjoy their children, instead of nagging them.

As a result, the family becomes a place where adults and children each have their own share of power and responsibility, a share appropriate to their age and position. For many children, this approach can ultimately lead to both better grades and an easier transition into adult life.

TEENS AND POWER

The wise use of power in the family can make the difference between chronic misery and maturity, especially with teenagers. Here is an alternative way of understanding power that can help parents avoid getting stuck in chronic power struggles.

Power is handed out unevenly in families, and on the surface it might seem as though adults get most of it. We're bigger and smarter, right? But, on the other hand, we all know families where the teenagers tie their parents up in knots.

In fact, the struggle for power is often most difficult at the stage when young people are developing that crucial ability to make their own decisions and possess both the independence and the vocabulary to score a few points.

Here is an example. It's a rainy day, so the parent, who knows well the negative effects of cold, wet feet, will say, "Don't go out without your boots, dear."

The teenager, who is equally aware of what is considered stylish this year, will say, "Forget it. I'm wearing my runners."

When things reach this point it is pretty tempting for a parent to turn the argument into something like a wrestling match, in other words, to try to force their antagonist to yield. With a teenager, this is both a very difficult proposition and, in any case, the kind of approach that usually results in a continuing power struggle.

"But if I have to nurse my kids through a cold or the flu," you may reply, "I have a right to make them wear boots." Fair enough. You have your rights. But keep in mind that you also have to make a choice between short- and long-term gains. In this case, the short-term choice is a possible virus, the long-term choice a certain and chronic power struggle.

So check out the alternative model for your disagreements: the martial arts of the Far East. Like the martial arts expert, parents can actually take advantage of their young opponent's weight and motion.

In short, you can struggle with your teen about footwear for years. Or you can stand back a little and allow the natural consequences of your teenagers' own decisions, those two cold, wet feet, to teach them how to dress for health and comfort.

It's all in the way you throw your weight around.

FIVE TASKS OF THE TEEN YEARS

When your easy-going children suddenly turn into opinionated, moody, rebellious teenagers, all at once you find yourselves desperately trying to keep calm and figure out what on earth this tumultuous stage is all about.

Dr. Esther Cole has identified the five tasks of the teen years. These are tasks that have evolved to help kids grow into adults, and to free parents from constantly having to monitor their teens' every move.

The first task for teenagers is to build up their own sense of self-esteem, instead of relying on their parents' support. They are learning to recognize and cherish their own value.

Example: your teen constantly rejects your suggestions. "You don't know anything," is the message you're picking up. But it's really, "I'm learning to trust me rather than depend on you."

The second task is finding out how to take care of themselves while not running all over everybody else. In this sense, the teen years resemble a marathon, seven-year, assertiveness training program, exhausting for all concerned.

Example: Your teen stays at a friend's place doing homework, instead of returning home in time for dinner. That's assertion. The next essential next stage is consideration: "Hi, it's Danny. I'm not going to be home for dinner with the family. I'll fix something for myself later." That will come in time.

The third task for teens is learning self-control, channelling their emotional energy, so that they don't dissipate it, but use it to achieve those things that they really want out of life.

Example: In their teens, your kids may stop telling you how they feel about the bumps and disappointments in their lives. They don't cry or laugh with you as much. They may seem distant and cold. But for them it's just a necessary part of not letting themselves get overwhelmed by their feelings.

Fourth, they are learning to think ahead about the dangers they may face in life, and figuring out what they'll do about them. After all, Mom and Dad, you won't always be there to hold their hands.

Example: "Don't pick me up at the school. Wait around the corner. I don't want the kids to think I'm a suck." Maybe that doesn't seem such a big danger to you, but it is the teen equivalent of a loaded dump truck coming at you with no brakes.

Finally, teens are becoming more selective about their friendships. That is an essential skill for independent adults, to be able to choose a circle of friends who will both support them and believe in them.

Example: You can't stand that boy your teenager is hanging around with. Definitely a bad influence. But if you have done your job well up to now, your children will learn to differentiate between friends who encourage their self-respect and those whose surface charms conceal a hurtful meanness of spirit.

Admittedly, it is easy as parents to become profoundly irritated by all the grief and struggles you must endure while your teens are growing up. But as they go through this stage, the best thing you can do for them is to strive to understand why they're doing what they have to do. And to keep right on loving them.

ADULT CHILDREN WHO DON'T LEAVE HOME

Parents often worry when their children can't wait to leave home in their late teens to share an apartment with friends and discover freedom.

They wonder if the kids will be okay on their own. How will they handle the temptations and assaults of a cruel world? What will they do when freedoms like sex turn into responsibilities?

These are legitimate concerns, but they may seem less dramatic when parents compare them with the opposite phenomenon, children in their twenties, often their late twenties, who are still living at home. That can cause major stress for everyone in the family.

When a teenager becomes a young adult, yet continues to live at home, it often strains family relationships because no one knows how to treat this child-who-is-no-longer-a-child. Mom and Dad are used to making the rules around the house, but now there is a full-blown adult living with them who wants to make his or her own decisions.

This situation is frequently a rough road for the older generation. There are 28-year-olds around whose parents lie awake on Friday nights until they are safely home. In other families, the parents still provide room and board at no cost, even though their adult child may be working full-time. This can pose a serious financial strain on them, and it may lead to a growing feeling of resentment.

Another worrisome possibility is that this arrangement may preoccupy the parents, providing a ready excuse for ignoring the need for growth in their own relationship at what should be a new stage of their lives.

But the most harmful effects are generally on the adult children. The comforts of life with Mom and Dad frequently dull the appetite for the adventure of living on their own.

Mom makes the bed. Dad brings home the bread.

As a result of this cozy relationship, these adult children experience no risk, and little preparation for an independent life. When they move into a love relationship, often later than others, their mates frequently come to see them as spoiled children, especially once the honeymoon period is over.

In some ethnic groups there is considerable support for unmarried adult children living at home, so this arrangement may work for a while, but in many other cases, especially in mainstream North America, it turns out to be harmful to both generations.

ECONOMICS KEEP ADULT CHILDREN AT HOME

The growing phenomenon of young people in their twenties staying at home with their parents, instead of moving out and making their own lives, has unmistakable economic causes.

Quite simply, because there are relatively few good jobs available for young people, many of them cannot afford to live on their own. Housing is expensive, and money is short.

They are forced to share their parents' home, despite the discomfort of having three or more adults in a family originally designed for two adults and some small children. But apart from urging them to get the best possible training for today's work world, there is little the older generation can do for this group, until sufficient housing comes on the market and the economy develops more and better-paying jobs.

But there is another, more subtle, cause for this phenomenon, which is that many of these young adults have been raised with all the goodies. They have come to expect that the basics of life include a car or two in the garage, compact disc players,

VCRs, pay TV, computers, microwave ovens, steak for dinner, and everything else that money can buy—their parents' money, that is.

It is easy to complain that these kids are too soft and expect too much. Parents need to remember that we have formed many of their values. In fact, we may have let them down as children by failing to remind them that, in their twenties, they would have to go out on their own, pull themselves up by their bootstraps, and live on a shoestring until they have made their own lives and their own homes.

THE EMOTIONAL TIES OF ADULT CHILDREN

The harsh economic reality of low-paying jobs, and the inflated expectations of middle-class young people, are only part of the pattern that deters young people from leaving home in their late teens or early twenties and seriously delaying their life task of growing up and out.

At least equally important as finances are the emotional factors, particularly their fear of that complex and difficult world out there. Clinging to their parents can represent a measure of safety for those who are especially insecure.

A less obvious factor is that the parents are in some cases highly dependent on their children to maintain their marriage. Without consciously knowing it, they may fear that if their child leaves home, they will be left to stare at each other, trapped in a relationship from which affection and passion have long since evaporated.

In such cases, without consciously knowing why, the child may be staying home to help keep the parents from facing that bankrupt marriage.

There is no simple cure for insecurities of this sort. But here are four simple steps for families who are concerned about their living arrangements and want to get themselves unstuck.

1. Whether you are the parent or the adult child, take some time to think privately about how you are helping maintain the status quo. Try to be completely honest with yourself. What's in it for you? What are the hidden costs?

2. Sit down with the others and discuss what you have been thinking about alone. Remember, there is no right and wrong

here, just something you want to work out together. So make sure everyone gets a respectful hearing.

3. Spend some time telling each other how you would like to be living two years from today. Once you and your family are clear about your goals, you will find that some solutions will begin to suggest themselves.

4. Make plans together to fulfil those goals, but remember not to expect too much of yourselves. You don't have to resolve the whole issue today. Just move a step at a time.

In fact, it may take your family several discussions to reach this stage. That's fine. The important thing is not the speed you are moving at, but the fact that you are in motion, for the benefit of the whole family.

AVOIDING THE SCORCHED-PARENT SYNDROME

We've all heard about various professional groups who get burned out—social workers, nurses, teachers. But by far the largest category of people at risk from burnout are parents.

If you're a parent, you probably have some experience of "burnout"; it's that nagging feeling that you can't take any more of parenting, of loving no matter what, of the lack of appreciation.

It may be the result of too many 4 a.m. feedings with a new baby. It may be that your child needs continual reminders to feed the cat. Or it may be that your teenager is constantly at war with you. After a while, you simply get worn out.

The problem with the term "burnout" is that it sounds so final, as though, like a charred scrap of paper, you are beyond recovery. Well, you may be a little charred but you are not ashes. So, just to keep a light-hearted perspective on the problem, we'll call it the Scorched-Parent Syndrome (SPS).

In case you still believe that burnout is some kind of fancy problem that only hits people who work outside the home, let me assure you that it happens very commonly to parents. The five-part definition of professional burnout which you will find below, explains why.

First of all, people who burn out are doing a job that is emotionally demanding.

That certainly describes parenting. Love, anger, anxiety, joy, sorrow—not one of them is foreign to the lives of mothers and fathers. Parents get plenty of emotional exercise, coping with everything from cuts and burns, lost children, lost toys, and temper tantrums to the little one's first steps, first words, report cards, loves, and graduations.

Second, burnout hits those who care a lot—sometimes too much—about the job and the people they work with.

You can't be a parent and not care. It is hard to stand back emotionally while your own flesh and blood go through their developmental stages. It is just as impossible to ignore their anger and rejection as it is to dismiss their affection. But the parents who suffer SPS are those who have not mastered the graceful skill of stepping back a pace or two at times and letting their child move on without them.

Third, those who burn out run into more challenges than they do rewards.

No question about it, parenting is often a thankless task. The kids didn't ask to be born, as they point out from time to time, usually when parents are at their most vulnerable. No, the adults started it all, so we have to give, give, give, whether or not anyone says thank you. What reward can possibly compensate for staying up to three with a sick infant or waiting up till two for a teenager who is past curfew?

Fourth, this situation continues for a long time.

What this means is that professionals who burn out have often been on the firing line for several years. It's a lot, but at least at the end of the day they generally get to go home. In parenting, the contract calls for 24-hours-a-day for 18 years at a minimum.

And fifth, as a result of all this, people suffering from professional burnout start feeling frantic at times, and totally apathetic at other times.

Do you recognize this one? Do you find yourself so wound up emotionally that you are unable to undo the knot? Be honest now; are there times when you wish the kids would take themselves for a very long walk?

If you fit this definition, you may be suffering from an ominous, but non-terminal, case of SPS. It's time to do something about it.

HEALING SCORCHED-PARENT SYNDROME

There is no job harder, or hotter, than parenting. For parents who are victims of the "Scorched-Parent Syndrome," and more than a little burnt around the edges, here are four practical ideas to help you cool the fire.

First of all, give yourself a rest. A holiday might be best. But even a couple of hours engrossed in a book, or getting out of a noisy house for a long walk, are a lot better for SPS sufferers than nothing at all.

Second, start negotiating with your husband, wife, or partner, about how you can share the parenting load better. Just because you tend to have better natural skills as a parent doesn't mean that you should do all the child care. Your partner can learn.

Third, find someone outside the situation to talk to, perhaps a friend who will listen to whatever you have to say about the kids without judging you.

Fourth, let go of your need for the kids a little. Instead of looking to them for your sense of satisfaction and well-being in life, shift the emphasis to your spouse and your other adult friends. You'll feel happier that way, and consequently you will become a much better parent.

Because of SPS, some parents lose their hope, their cheer, and their enjoyment of life. Now you know better.

FOLLOW YOUR DREAM, SON

"It is far better that you like yourself just the way you are than that you try to twist yourself into some unnatural shape in the hope of buying my approval."

I had a chat the other day with my eleven-year-old son, and what I said to him is one of my favourite themes, whether I'm talking with children or working with my adult clients.

I told him, "If you have a dream, go for it."

As I talked with him, I was thinking of times in my life when I have allowed other people to define who I am. Times when I failed to cherish my own ideals, fantasies, and dreams, and even my own quirky character. Times when I wasted my vital energy trying to fit, like a round peg, into a square hole designed by somebody else.

What makes this too-common behaviour so crazy is the way we persist with it, even though it never really works. For whenever people are "good" or "nice" in an attempt to buy the approval of others, especially members of their families, and above all their parents, their anger level grows inexorably higher.

Many children who fear confrontation demonstrate their anger in sneaky ways. Not only do they become bitter and resentful toward others, stealing, for instance, or teasing younger kids, but at the same time, they may turn their anger inward, becoming sullen, withdrawn, and depressed, and often failing at school. It is no way to live.

And that is why I said to my son: "Be who you are, follow your dreams. In the process, you may upset me or others a little, but we will recover. And you, my son, will thrive."

CHAPTER EIGHT

Business and Career

Many people who have done well in business, the arts, or other demanding jobs, are disturbed by a nagging suspicion that their home life is suffering by neglect. They love their children and spouses, and know they deserve more from them. At times they are struck by a sudden recognition of the years rolling by, while their families drift further and further away.

If all they had to do, to make it better, was to take the occasional afternoon off and walk the kids to the park, they would do it. But they are torn, because of career responsibilities which include pulling a fair share of the weight at work. In some cases, thousands of others depend on their leadership to make the work place profitable. And they are doubly bound, because, in many cases, their families have grown demanding, expecting that they will both spend more time with them and bring home more and more of the bacon.

YOUR AT-HOME PERFORMANCE APPRAISAL

"Terrific," some folks mutter to themselves after undergoing a blowup at home. "I'm a roaring success at work, but when it comes to the family, I'd have to rate myself barely competent."

If you are the kind of person who wants to achieve as good a Performance Appraisal for your home life as you get at work, here are four categories to check.

ONE: YOUR PITCH-IN RATING

The high-performance spouse is prepared to pitch in at home. He or she knows that there is no such thing as love without hard work.

Babies, to take a small example, are great to cuddle and play with, but they also need their smelly diapers changed. It is a worn-out fallacy that love means never having to say, "I'll diaper."

If you imagine that just because of your important career, you can be a fun-time mom or dad, and escape the chores, you are kidding yourself. The all-seeing household accounting department is constantly vigilant, and in fact, you are risking considerable resentment from your partner, who knows when you are not pulling your weight.

TWO: YOUR SELF-CARE RATING

On the other hand, you do have a right to get your own needs met at home. For instance, lots of folk arrive home utterly frazzled from the office, the city, and the traffic jams. So if you happen to function best following 15 quiet minutes with the newspaper, fair enough. Negotiate to have that break before you are expected to pitch in.

But if you find you are letting those 15 minutes stretch to half-an-hour, then you are just begging for more resentment. Whether you intend it or not, you are sending an unmistakable message that you don't consider family responsibilities a high priority. Duck.

You do have a right, and in fact a need, for time to yourself: to go for a walk, to work out, or even to stare at the wall. In fact, you are much more likely to score a high pitch-in rating at home if you are also watching your self-care rating.

By the same reasoning, you will want to make sure your partner enjoys equal opportunities.

THREE: YOUR QUALITY-TIME RATING

One sure way of getting a superior Domestic Performance Appraisal is to spend some quality time every day with both the children and your mate.

One caution: don't kid yourself that you are being generous when you donate some of your quality time to other members of your family. The truth is that quality time with your loved ones is an essential aspect of your own self-care.

There is no question that it will make them happy, but essentially this is a very selfish act. It is simply good for your soul.

Sometimes people find that word, "quality," confusing, so let's have a look at its meaning.

It means moments when any two or more of you experience a deeper level of contact with each another, compared to those occasions when you just happen to be in the same space at the same time; for instance, sitting silently watching TV or driving through heavy traffic.

The more obvious examples of quality time include chatting as you eat a meal together around the table, going for a walk, or simply sitting and talking about your experiences since you saw each other last. Remember, if your spouse has been at home with children, he or she may desperately need another adult to talk to and consult about the events of the day.

But the idea of quality time can also include momentary experiences: like a loving hand on the shoulder, a tiny gift, a kiss and a hug at bedtime, a query about an event in someone's life today, a bandage on a minor scrape, or the reminder "Hey, I love you."

Moments like this, minute though they may be, and fragile as a spider's thread, can in time form the beautiful, strong web of a child's self-esteem, or a mate's commitment.

The idea of quality time is not limited to the examples above. Paradoxically, it can also include watching TV or driving in heavy traffic, changing diapers or a lightbulb, preparing supper together, or even having a fight, as long as you both understand that these are merely context. The key thing in quality time is your love for each other.

FOUR:YOUR PRIORITIES RATING

One valuable step to a superior Home Life Appraisal is to check out your priorities about worklife and homelife. It rarely comes to this point, but, in a crunch when you have to choose, which one gets your best attention?

Career people who possess staying power, who have long-term creativity, are generally those who regard their family as the stabilizing, life-giving context within which their work and other aspects of their lives occur. Their families are as crucial to their success as the air they breathe.

Increasingly, even the most demanding employers are coming to understand this too. There is probably more concern about the family in the boardrooms of business than ever before.

So check out how you meet your own standards on the domestic scene.

Appraise yourself.

FALLING IN LOVE WITH A SEXY JOB

The quest for success at work is extremely seductive. So when it comes to a choice between that and home life, quite a few people give their hearts to their jobs.

Why? The major reason is that their jobs feel sexier than their relationships. They find it a turn-on to tackle a challenge at the office, resolve it, get a reward, and move on. Home life is rarely that simple, and that is why more people commit adultery with their jobs than with other human beings.

The most seductive thing about a sexy job is that it rarely demands the same level of commitment as home life. Like an affair with a stranger, it has a certain glamour, unencumbered by such expectations as undying love or even tenderness.

As well, the actual relationships with people at work are nowhere near as challenging as those at home. True, they may include feelings like tension, loyalty, and admiration, but those feelings are generally less complex than those complicated emotions of the home, which evoke so much human vulnerability: jealousy, anger, fear, and love.

Furthermore, apart from the locker rooms of professional athletes and the stages of strip-tease artists, there are few places of work where people actually have to take their clothes off in front of others.

That may seem a little obvious, but think about it. Nobody at the office is going to assess your flesh close-up, examine that little roll of fat, or notice those stretch marks. You can carry on an affair with your career and never have to undress. Not so with a real live lover, not so with a real live spouse.

Physical nakedness is one thing, but as far as emotional nakedness is concerned—an even more difficult proposition—a career never asks a tenth of the openness that successful home life absolutely demands.

Because being so open makes people pretty vulnerable, they are sometimes hurt by their partners and often frightened of being hurt. For protection, they may cover themselves up emotionally at home, and sneak out to the office, where it is more acceptable to keep their feelings under wraps.

After a while, the spouses of career lovers begin to sense that something has gone wrong. But they are often slow to get angry and demand fidelity when the paramour is a desk or a production line. This kind of affair is often so subtle it takes a long time to notice.

So you, in fact, may be the only one to catch on.

In the end, what it comes down to is not lust but personal courage. When a seductive career beckons, do you have the wisdom to keep it at arm's length, and the daring to give your heart instead to a real, complex, demanding human being?

CAREER SUCCESS: MARRIAGE TROUBLE

People who devote their lives wholeheartedly to business success, and, as they put it, trying to provide the best for their families, may make it big in terms of salary and position, but too often when they reach their forties and fifties, the bottom falls out of their lives.

I'm not talking about being fired or let go, though that in itself is often a worry. No, the whole notion of loyalty to the job begins to look like some kind of cruel joke when, to their surprise, they find themselves alone, their marriages in ruins and their children remote strangers.

One such man is Malcolm. He is a senior executive with a highly respected firm. He is upwardly mobile and capable, and everybody at work likes him. So why, today, is this mover and shaker in tears?

The answer, he says, is that he doesn't get much satisfaction from his work anymore. Sure, he says, he's good at it, but it all seems so meaningless. The success he strove so hard to reach is hollow now. And the one thing he does care about, his marriage, is in trouble.

Well, you can guess how it got that way. Like many executives, Malcolm's single-minded dedication to success meant that back home his wife got the short end of the stick.

Most nights, he brought his work home from the office, and when he wasn't working, he was so tired he just wanted a little peace and quiet—with the TV, that is.

After a while, his wife started looking around for a man who would bring his heart and mind home from the office, not just a tired body and a loaded briefcase.

When he discovered her affair, he fell apart for awhile. However, the forecast for Malcolm and his wife is now guardedly optimistic. Because his wife is less disloyal than lonely, she seems open to trying to turn their marriage around.

And because Malcolm badly wants to reassess his priorities and learn to communicate, he has already begun really to pay attention to her, to listen to her feelings as well as her words.

A possible pitfall Malcolm faces is that he will have to convince her that he is serious about her as a person, not simply running from his unhappiness at work. That will require endurance and dedication.

But, on the plus side, like many men and women his age, Malcolm now wants more than anything else, even more than business success, to make a happy marriage.

CAREER SUCCESS: FAMILY TROUBLE

Few goals in corporate society are more appealing than making it to the top of the ladder. But as many working parents are discovering, success in business at any price can be far too high a price to pay.

Look at Kenneth, for example, who has risen steadily through a major multinational corporation, until now, in his late forties, he is very near the top.

As usual, this success took a lot of late nights and weekends at the office. As a result, these days, his teenage kids hardly seem to know him. To them, he is just the distracted old stranger with the grey suit and the briefcase who happens to live at their house.

Mom, on the other hand, is usually around, and although she and Dad don't seem to have much in common, and she doesn't seem very happy, at least the children can count on her for interest and advice. So they remain unusually close to her.

Well, you can see the problems developing for the children. Because they have missed their prime opportunity to learn to relate intimately with an adult male, they may always have difficulties developing close relationships with men.

Having become at the same time overdependent on a female, there is a real danger, for boys in particular, that they may focus a disproportionate amount of their attention on women, resenting, using, or abusing them.

Not the best preparation for adult life and relationships.

And Kenneth? Well, having reached the top, he has found that when you get there, it turns out not to be what you wanted after all.

As he looks ahead to early retirement on a generous pension, all he can see is loneliness and time on his hands. His marriage may not make it, or maybe it will, but one thing is sure: his kids are not likely to flock around him.

This withering away of family life was once an exclusively male problem. But today's ambitious professional women should also heed the warning implicit in Kenneth's story.

Otherwise, the high price of their success may also be paid by them and by their families.

SUCCESSFUL BUSINESSES SHARE THE POWER

As the business environment becomes more competitive, many old-style managers feel deeply frustrated. They have discovered that if they try to squeeze more productivity out of their workers, they often get the opposite result.

But the so-called "excellent" corporations have already done the basic research into better ways of handling their people and one of their findings is that our belief in bigger-is-better is a mistake.

For example, as recently as the early 1970s, the Ford Motor Company decided to build itself an enormous engine factory, the size of 72 football fields. And then? Well, then they had to shut it down, because it was just too big and alienating.

In the 1980s, we are beginning to rediscover the alternatives to "bigness." These new approaches have helped transform reluctant, resistant workers into committed and creative successes; so far, one of the best ideas tested in the pursuit of excellence is the decentralization of power.

The old-style management approach of large corporations used to be to concentrate power in a central head office. From there instructions were sent out into the field, to ensure that the job got done properly. But that approach constantly ran afoul of human nature, clashing with people's natural tendency to resist authority when it imposes arbitrary rules.

Today's new style—with its roots in Japan—puts together small teams of managers and employees out in the field where the work is actually done, to take responsibility for the product together. They're called "quality circles," and they operate like little companies within the larger corporation.

The key to their enormous success is simple: because everyone feels a stake in the outcome, most team members work harder and use their imagination to get the job done more efficiently.

Sharing the responsibility with their workers does not come easily to managers whose eyes are nervously scanning the bottom line. It is understandably hard to let go of power, especially when the stakes are very high and the level of trust between managers and workers is correspondingly low.

But, proceeding with due caution and more than a little anxiety, a new generation of progressive managers are encouraging "small," and opting for relationships with their workers that actually increase their competitive edge.

ATTITUDE CAN HELP SOLVE BUSINESS CRISES

Beginning with Japan, the industries of the Far East have flooded North America with better, cheaper, products: cars, cameras, and computers, to name just a few.

Unfortunately, when North American businesses are crowded out of the market by the quality and price of products from Asia and other parts of the world, their reaction is not a positive one.

Like their governments, the first reaction of many of our chief executive officers is a power move.

They may get tough with their workers, cut benefits, or freeze salaries, all in the hope of remaining competitive. The result is, of course, totally predictable: resentful, uncommitted employees, who continue to under-produce and are now tempted to sabotage the product. In other words, a downward spiral.

This approach fails because it is adversarial, archaic, and, in terms of human relations, bankrupt.

What our corporate heads need is to look at another Far Eastern import, the attitude that made their success possible.

This common-sense alternative draws out the best in human nature. In this model, the attitude is: "We're all in this together, and that is how we'll get out of it too—whether we're presidents, members of the board, managers, operators, or clerical or cleaning staff."

This is no clever public relations campaign, designed by management to seduce their employees into harder work for less reward. That has already been tried, and found wanting. No, this is a significant change of attitude which is beginning to turn our industrial sector upside down.

This attitude begins with enlightened chief executives who communicate their vision to their employees, and filters down through management (whose most difficult task may be shucking off their old attitudes to leadership). Then—and only then—it shows results in the work and attitudes of the working people

It rests on the realization that both management and workers are highly vulnerable in our volatile market. And that despite their differing roles, they share similar interests: job security, good wages, and a product that is satisfying to create and to market.

We don't have to go to Japan these days to find ready proof that when employees and management pull together, the results are excellent, for them and for the public which purchases their goods.

These principles are just as applicable, certainly equally crucial, to volunteer organizations and small businesses, and even to the home and the family. They work for groups of any size, not because they are derived from clever theories, but because they are based on fundamental principles of human personality and human interaction.

A NEW BUSINESS PERSPECTIVE ON HOMELIFE

As successful businesses take an up-to-date look at their employees, they have found that those who have a solid, happy homelife provide their companies with a measurable, dollars-and-cents payback.

Unfortunately, some of the attitudes of the Industrial Revolution still persist. In those days, as the manufacturing industries came on stream, adults and even children were treated as units of labour, without regard for their physical health or relationships. Employees were worked to exhaustion, and then discarded and replaced.

Of course, today's businesses are more humane and more conservative. Most are deeply concerned about the health and welfare of their employees, and committed to conserving their strength and capability.

Yet in most firms there remains a vast pool of old-style managers, many of whom were originally promoted from the shop floor. These are people who have learned about management only in the school of hard knocks and have received no formal human relations training.

While some of them have turned out to possess an innate talent for managing people effectively, tragically too many of them are desperately naive.

For instance, it is not uncommon for these supervisors to believe that their major duty is to wring every available ounce of work out of their subordinates. If that happens to result in some fallout in the employee's homelife, well, they may say to themselves, that is not their problem. After all, that is how they were treated when they worked on the shop floor.

Only with adequate training for their jobs can they understand that those employees who neglect their relationships at home will ultimately cost their companies time and money. Only with adequate and encouraging support from their senior management will they feel free to adapt new managerial habits that encourage family life.

They may need some help at first grappling with the more subtle equations. For example, when the employee's family know that, in the long haul, they come first, they can be remarkably tolerant, even supportive, if a short-term job crisis demands extra hours at the workplace.

Those who come to understand human relations know that workers who put family life first—whether they're presidents or sweepers—stay healthier, work better, and last longer.

A NEW UNDERSTANDING OF MANAGEMENT

The most effective companies on this continent are those who regard their workers not as "just another pair of hands," but as important individuals, whose ideas and human commitment are essential to corporate success.

Generally, such attitudes originate in the executive boardrooms. But it is management whose job it is to convert executive dreams into production line realities.

As a result, in today's "excellent" organizations, the most valued managers are those who know how to encourage people. Above all, they are motivators, with the skill to communicate the company's values to their increasingly well-educated and thoughtful employees. Such managers help transform workers from drudges into heroes.

One of the ways they motivate is by understanding that their people have a need for control over their own lives. So these managers share the power.

For instance, instead of assigning the task of quality control to an isolated department, they make every worker his or her own quality inspector. In fact, for the motivated worker, quality control becomes a state of mind.

A hundred years ago, Karl Marx pointed out that the workers' sense of alienation from their workplace and its products was the key to the growing problems between labour and management. Ironically, it has taken us a full century of labour strife to begin to comprehend his diagnosis, but now a number of leading organizations are actually demonstrating a cure for alienation.

The essential ingredient in this aspect of corporate success is a management group with good interpersonal skills, a group who can translate respect for the worker from precept to practice.

THE SPLIT BETWEEN HOME AND WORK

For many people, career and home life are as different as night and day, although each person defines that difference in a personal way. For one, business is creativity, and home is comfort. For another, business is tough city, while home is a place for love.

So they may picture themselves as two different people: the coolly efficient work person, and the emotional family person.

What many working people fail to notice, however, is that the single thread which runs through both locations is their personality. And while the curtains may be drawn over it a little more at work than at home, personality is their greatest strength and drawback in both locations.

FORCES BEYOND HIS CONTROL

George gave every outward sign of being a success. In fact, his education, cleverness, and organizational ability had landed him a significant job in the corporation.

On the other hand, at home he was the picture of insecurity, fearful of asserting himself with his wife, lacking in confidence as a parent, and occasionally petulant—all in all desperately unhappy.

Some people think of work and home as two different worlds, but, like George, most employees carry a great deal of emotional baggage every time they travel back and forth between them.

So perhaps his unhappiness at home was not so strange when contrasted with his success at work as it might seem. In fact, if you had asked those at work who knew him best, they might have told you much the same thing as his wife.

"George is highly competent," they might say, "but he lacks guts. He's got all the credentials, but there's something missing inside."

Working at a level where team confidence is essential, they might add, "We don't quite trust George. You never quite relax with him. He has terrific ideas, but he can also be dangerous.

"On the other hand, he's very easy to intimidate, so he often gets used by those who report to him."

Because of those qualities, George was the kind of manager who is vulnerable during cuts in personnel. He knew this, and because he could never quite relax and feel secure at the office, his edgy qualities became all the more abrasive.

People like George, when they're not lucky, get fired—or, worse still, hang on miserably for decades. When they're lucky, they are pressured to make changes as a condition of secure employment.

But when they are neither lucky, nor unlucky, but simply smart, they do what George did. He began to discuss his anxiety with himself. He explored various possibilities: that his bosses were prejudiced, that his firm had no concern for its employees, that the people he supervised were plotting against him.

Ultimately, he recognized that he himself had to be the problem, and he started on the painful task of understanding his own makeup. Determined to be in control of his life, rather than a victim of emotional forces outside his control, he began to draw himself into one whole person.

What emerged, very gradually, was something that till then, neither George nor his co-workers would ever have predicted. It was the discovery that the route to his business development ran through his home life.

Gradually, he began to assert himself at home. He asked for more from his family, but he gave more too. He began to dismantle the rigid structures of self-protection that kept him a stranger there, and showed himself as a more vulnerable, and indeed a more appealing person.

As he made changes at home, his professional associates gradually became aware of the shift in his personality. One of them, who knew nothing about George's inner process, said it was as though he were "filling out." Far from jeopardizing any of his intellectual ability, he was adding emotional strength to his business capabilities.

The process was not easy. It took many months and much dedication. Only those who knew him best even guessed that he was reworking his entire approach to human relations.

But in the end he began to feel to his co-workers like someone strong enough to be confronted rather than intimidated. They found themselves more relaxed around him. And without anyone actually saying anything about it, he dropped off the unspoken "We'll have to get rid of him eventually" list.

None of this did his home life any harm either, but then that's another story.

FAMILY LIFE AND THE WORK PLACE

Business has always recognized the importance of family life.

Without family life, there would have been no women at the corporate cocktail parties, no humanizing photos of "the kids" on otherwise sterile desks, no one to cook dinner for important out-of-town guests.

Much of that is gradually changing now, as many women reject the role of "corporate wife."

Beyond that, the connections between family life and career success are in the process of being redefined. Today, knowing that family life is the context within which business operates, rather than the other way around, we see how it affects performance.

The home is a climate, an environment: and it makes a big difference whether an employee comes into work relaxed by gentle sunny days, stimulated by the gusty wind, excited by the beauty of sparkling snow, or, on the other hand, exhausted from fighting through a storm, shivering from the cold, fried by the merciless sun, frightened and lonely in the midst of lightning.

Of course, in the same sense, the work world is also an powerful environment affecting home life, but its effects are rarely as powerful, because a career lacks the primal connections of family.

Family is primal. It was within a family that each of us developed our personality. For good or for ill, and usually for both, family life shaped our adult strengths and vulnerabilities.

It may possibly be different for those raised in the wilds by wolves or dolphins, but all the rest of us carry "family" around with us like the photos in our wallets—only closer to the heart.

There are no exceptions. Even those few who are unmated, childless, friendless, totally isolated from their brothers, sisters, and parents, even they bring their family into work with them every single day. In a multitude of ways, the quality of their childhood relationships with siblings and parents will influence every interaction with their co-workers.

That is why the person who has never struggled to understand his or her relationships with his or her family, past and present, is automatically limited to amateur status when it comes to understanding relationships at work.

CHAPTER NINE

Separation and Divorce

In the dark distant past, a man could divorce his wife simply by saying "I divorce you" three times. This charming custom persists in some parts of the world to this day. Of course, women have generally lacked this privilege, but as the centuries passed, obtaining a divorce became tougher for everyone, in some countries even requiring an act of Parliament.

Today, for every two marriages in the United States and Canada, there is likely to be one divorce. While statistics may fluctuate slightly up and down in any given period, there is no sign of a letup. Over a million North American children will experience divorce this year. Reckon into this picture as well the growing number of separating couples who escape the statisticians by living together unmarried. If we ever needed evidence that today's marriages are fragile, we have it now.

The only significant question remaining is this: if this disaster should strike, are there ways to make a peace between the two adults, to end a marriage without rancor?

SOME HELP FOR PARENTS FACING SEPARATION

When a couple decide they have to break up, it is often frightening and painful to inform the adult members of their families. But the hardest part of all, they may find, is telling the children.

Some separating couples put off informing their kids for weeks and months. The sad, and ironic, reality is that at some level, their children already know that a terrible event is looming. Even little toddlers know. But if the adults have given them no facts as guidelines, their young minds will conjure up anxieties far worse than reality.

They have two overwhelming fears:

First, "It's my fault. It's something I did that made them angry at each other. If I'm very, very good, maybe if I keep my room tidier, they'll be happy again."

This fear is based on children's magical sense of power. Because their young minds don't distinguish easily between adult problems and their own actions, they carry the overwhelming burden of their own imagined omnipotence.

Second, most children fear for their future. "If Mommy and Daddy don't love each other, I won't have a place to live. And then I'll be all by myself."

This pitiful dread derives from a contrary reality, the sense of utter powerlessness that haunts children. To an adult mind, the notion of abandonment may seem to contradict their magical sense of omnipotence, but in children's minds there is plenty of room for internal inconsistency.

These often unspoken twin terrors constitute the reason that parents have to put aside their anxiety, face facts, and tell their children what is actually going on.

Children of all ages need to hear, over and over again, the corresponding reassurances:

First, that none of their parents' unhappiness is their fault. They didn't cause it. And they cannot fix it.

Second, that Mommy and Daddy will always love them, and as long as they are children, they will always have a place to live with one or both of their parents.

MESSAGE TO A SEPARATED DAD

This is for Benjamin's father. Last week, your eight-year-old son sat in my office looking like the world had come to an end.

Ever since you and your wife split up, Benjamin has always looked forward to spending Sundays with you. He would wait around near the front door, looking so proud and happy, "Cuz my dad is gonna take me to his place."

But he has been in pretty rough shape since you had that fight about support payments with his mother. The fight that ended with you saying angrily that you were not coming to get Benjamin on Sundays any more.

I think I understand your feelings. You're exasperated and hurt with all the discord. You and your wife are so raw from breaking up that it is easy for your disagreements to turn into major battles.

But if you're hurting, Dad, your son is in agony. He is wondering if it was something he did that made his dad not love him anymore.

His mother has tried to explain that it is not his fault. But he can't concentrate at school and he is miserable at home. This little boy has just run into his second major crisis in two years, and he is beginning to come apart.

Dad, you can make all that better.

I understand that you have adult problems; well, keep them between the adults. If you two can't cope with them, and an angry separation is one of the hardest situations to handle without help, don't feel ashamed to see a divorce mediator.

The point is that right now your little boy needs a father, and if he doesn't get one soon, the scars will affect him all his life.

Won't you phone Benjamin today, and tell him that you'll be there, next Sunday morning, as usual?

THE CRISIS OF DESPAIR

When adult relationships come to an unhappy end, when separation tears a couple apart, or a family is shredded by anger, the people involved find themselves in the midst of a complex crisis. Not only are they faced with major practical tasks, like finding a new home and new relationships; the most intimidating hurdle some have to face is the crisis of despair.

Despair shows itself when a separated father suddenly stops his weekly visits to his son, who until then has been the light of his life. Here is a man grieving the loss of a marriage, and then, in his hopelessness, separating himself from his one remaining, dependable source of open-hearted love, his own child.

Or consider the prominent judge, so wise in administering the counsels of justice, who splits up with his wife and then hands everything he has over to her—the house, the car, the savings— leaving himself broke, as if his own needs were of no account at all. These are the actions of a guilt-ridden man who has lost his expectation of a meaningful future.

These reactions to crisis seem extreme, but if you were to examine the lives of these otherwise dynamic, capable people prior to their separations, you might have glimpsed subtle evidence of despair. You might have watched as they allowed an unhappy relationship to continue neither challenged nor treated, or looked on as they wounded their partners with angry words, where healing was needed.

Although this hopelessness may never have appeared full-blown before, people like these have often experienced events during childhood that somehow strangled their self-esteem, and so, their faith in life. What remained for adulthood was only a plodding determination to get through their days with the least possible pain, an attitude which contributes to the breakdown of their relationships and threatens to entrap them forever in negativity.

I wish I could say that such people are exceptional. But in fact, there are so many of them, self-stuck in dead-end attitudes, dead-end jobs, dead-end relationships, and sometimes dead-end solitude.

If you are one of them, it is time to confront depression and hopelessness. You were created for more than this, created for inner joy and intimate relationships. Don't let despair hold you back. Reach out for life.

No one else can do this for you, but once you decide you want to be open to life, there is more help and guidance available than ever before in the history of the world. You can heal your wounds, even wounds of despair that date from childhood, with the almost unlimited assistance available through books, tapes, self-help groups, spiritual traditions, and mental health professionals.

Nobody has to go it alone, no one who really wants to grow.

So talk to trusted friends and members of your family. Tell them that you are struggling with hopelessness. Some of them will know the various resources available, and help you evaluate them, as you turn to your own healing.

And if you have a friend or relative who seems to be in despair, remember that you might be just the person who can be a therapist to this friend. You don't need a degree or a clever spiel. A listening, non-judgmental ear is all your friend or relative needs from you.

GOOD GUYS AND GUILTY PARTIES

A major factor in how well people cope with the breakdown of relationships is the attitude of our society. Unfortunately, there are still lots of folks around who, whenever something goes wrong, feel an overwhelming need to blame somebody.

Anybody will do. It just helps these folks avoid thinking about their own faults.

These are the kind whose view of life is neat and simple, complete with good guys and so-called "guilty parties." They find it a very tidy way to look at life.

However reality is rarely so orderly, and the truth about marriage breakdown, as therapists and researchers have consistently found, is considerably more complex. It takes two people, not one, to make a marriage, and, in the vast majority of cases, the same number to wreck it.

That makes assigning the blame not nearly as easy as it was.

Gradually, public attitudes to marriage breakdown are changing. Today many people understand that people who divorce are not evil, or even "strange"—merely tragic.

Our laws, simply reflections of public attitudes, were once highly punitive in their attitudes to alimony and the custody of children. Today they too are in the midst of change, discouraging an adversarial approach and offering better assistance, even comfort, to that very large minority in our society who are personally affected by divorce.

IN-LAWS BECOMING OUT-LAWS

It is very painful for the parents of adult children to watch helplessly while their kids' marriages break up. In many cases, they have no warning that trouble is brewing. They are shocked by the sudden anger and emotional violence within their family. They feel saddened, hurt, and then often angry themselves.

So how should they respond?

The most important advice is to stand back a little. Your children need love and support, but they don't need you to take sides.

For example, last year Reg and Harriet's daughter-in-law walked out on their son. Their first reaction was to phone her, several times in fact, to tell her that she was making a serious mistake. When that didn't work, they tried to make her feel guilty about how much she had hurt their grandchildren. Finally, they refused to talk to her at all.

In a sense, their behaviour was not so surprising. It was their way of expressing their concern, their loyalty, even their love.

The irony is that while couples like this may reconcile with each other, they might never again trust or forgive their meddling in-laws.

And even if separation does end in divorce, that blaming attitude can deeply hurt the separating couple. The last thing they need is more angry, interfering people around than they already have.

In either case, they are liable to treat their in-laws from henceforth as out-laws.

A caution: if you are tempted to get involved and take sides, keep in mind that in virtually every case the situation is actually far more complicated than you will ever know.

In Reg and Harriet's case, for instance, the knowledge they lacked was far more than what they had. No one, in fact, had ever seen what happened between their son and daughter-in-law behind closed doors. No one knew that his cruel digs and constant criticism had left her an emotional wreck. No one knew that her old confidence was in shreds. And no one, apart from her closest friends, recognized that walking out on him was the first step in rebuilding her self-esteem.

So parents, and friends too, put your judgments on hold. Assume there's more to it than meets the eye.

Your best approach is to stand back a little, and, however you can do it, be prepared to support these two hurting people.

THE CHALLENGE OF DIVORCED PARENTING

When two people separate, their family, in the conventional sense of the word, breaks up too. Suddenly, the old family models no longer fit the situation, but the children still need parenting.

So the adults have to find new ways to parent their children. For decades, our society has assumed that the mother would have sole custody, and the father visiting rights. She would stay at home and care for the children, while he moved out and supported the family from afar. But our attitudes are changing, as we get the benefit of up-to-date research.

Except in a few cases involving serious abuse, many thoughtful professionals now believe that "shared parenting" is best for children, because it keeps both parents involved in their lives. Too often we have watched fathers (and occasionally mothers) who are stripped of all connection with their children except for financial support and occasional visits. These peripherial parents gradually get discouraged, as they feel less and less involved in the raising of their own children.

That situation hurts everyone. The visiting parent loses contact with the children, and the parent with custody loses the potential help and support of the other parent.

Above all, the children suffer incalculable losses: the love, the day-to-day care, the physical contact, and the role-model of the parent who has only visiting rights.

Even though particular marriages may not survive, parenthood is forever. Perhaps the children will end up living with both parents alternately, perhaps with only one. Either way, wise divorced parents behave in certain recognizable ways. They encourage the children to spend time with the ex-spouse, keep each other informed about what is happening in the kids' lives, and make crucial decisions together, decisions on topics such as health care, education, vocation, religion, and relationships.

There are, of course, disadvantages. It is understandable that some would prefer never to talk with their ex-spouse again. It is difficult when your ideas and values differ, as inevitably they will.

But it is entirely worth the frustration and annoyance you suffer, because of the benefit to the children of having two fully-involved parents in their lives.

HELPING THE CHILDREN THROUGH THE BREAKUP

When a marriage breaks up, everyone worries if the children will be scarred for life, or whether they will live happier ever after. In fact, many unhappy couples stay together just to avoid finding out.

If you are going through a separation, you probably wonder how you can make certain that your children aren't damaged. The truth, I'm afraid, is that you can't.

But there are at least four ways you can minimize the harm and help them recover from this traumatic event:

I have already mentioned the first rule: make sure that both parents stay actively involved in the children's lives, except in the rare cases where one parent is actually dangerous.

The second is to limit the number of transitions the children have to cope with. One little girl, caught in the midst of a split up, screeched out, "There are too many changes!" For the sake of her emotional security, she needed to stay in the same school and live in the same house for awhile, even though eventually the family would have to move.

Third, kids need to know that the same old family rules still apply. They will test the new situation in dozens of ways, limited only by their imagination and nerve: trying to stay up late, stealing, having tantrums, breaking precious decorations, avoiding chores, to list only a few. But they will feel more secure when they realize that they can't get away with manipulating their parents through guilt. Nor can they play one off against the other.

But the fourth, and most important, thing you need to know is that, whatever the changes in family life, there is no substitute— and never will be—for the old-fashioned qualities of love and affection. The child to worry about is the child who feels abandoned. The one who is given time, attention, and a gentle touch will usually do just fine.

THE RAW EMOTIONS THAT GO WITH SEPARATION

When couples decide they have to separate, it is usually because they are miserably unhappy. But in many cases that misery is nothing compared to the emotional turmoil that is on the way.

True, there are a few people who feel only a wonderful sense of relief when they end a painful marriage. But for most, the relief is mixed with less pleasant emotions.

They may feel a deep sadness, because of the loss of their hopes and dreams, and the loss of a person who was once very important to them.

They may be angry because of how the other person treated them.

Frequently they will have a powerful sense of guilt. They may blame themselves for the failure of a marriage, and they may wonder whether they tried hard enough. If they have children, they are probably all too aware of how much they are suffering.

As a result of all this raw feeling, recently separated people often do not cope very well with the ordinary stresses of life. They may be emotionally volatile. They may appear to be distant, or in a daze. These apparently "abnormal" states are actually quite normal, given what they are going through.

That is why if you are in the process of ending a marriage, you owe it to yourself to make sure you have someone trustworthy to talk with about your feelings.

And if you are a friend or relative of people who are separating, the best favour you can do them is to accept their idiosyncrasies, offer your support, and have faith that they will be better soon.

ASKING THE RIGHT QUESTIONS

The decision to get married is, for many people, remarkably quick and uncomplicated. But making the decision to get divorced can be slow and agonizing torture. In fact, some people delay that decision for years.

Here are some important questions for people who are contemplating ending their marriages, questions that may help you clarify your situation:

First of all, why is this relationship not working? Is it because it hasn't been getting the attention it deserves, because of outside stresses like overwork, ill health, and financial problems? Or is it because you are profoundly unhappy with your mate as a person? The former is a problem that can often be solved; the latter is more difficult.

If the problem is your partner's character, is he or she capable of change? And what about you? Are you part of the problem? (The inevitable answer is "Yes.") How willing are you to make changes?

Are you dying in this relationship, or simply bored and restless? Could you be satisfied with minor improvements? Or do you need substantial change to be able to survive the next decade?

Sometimes marriages sink because they have been torpedoed by inescapable major life events. A business failure, a life-changing illness, a forced move. Other times, couples simply drift into unhappiness and then drift into separation. Are you two drifting? If so, how could you halt the drift? Do you want to?

There is a silly story about a man whose donkey was said to be the hardest worker in the country. A neighbour borrowed it for a month, on the strength of its reputation, but returned it within a few days, complaining angrily that the donkey wouldn't work at all. At that, the owner picked up a two-by-four and whacked the donkey across the nose. "Why did you do that," asked the neighbour in a shocked voice. "Because first," the owner replied quietly, "you have to get its attention."

I don't recommend the use of two-by-fours, but there is no question that it often takes a shock to get couples moving. What would happen if you told your partner you see a divorce on the horizon? What if you walked out? Would it help you to halt the drift, to get his or her attention?

What if you and your partner were to agree to take a long, hard look at your marriage. Would that give the two of you a good scare? Would it motivate you to make it better?

Does the idea of separation seem less frightening or less arduous than confronting your problems together?

If you were to split, what would you miss most?

What if divorce cost you your comfortable standard of living? How much do you value that, compared with your emotional welfare?

What if it cost you a supportive relationship with your spouse's family?

What if you lost friends, or lost work?

If you don't separate, will it affect your overall well-being? Will life continue on much the same? Or will you then slowly die as a personality?

If you have someone else in your love life, is that person distracting you from putting all your energy into your marriage? What is his or her function? Providing a little excitement, a few hours of distraction from a miserable homelife? Representing the things you dream of within marriage? Reminding you that your marriage needs work?

How is your energy level? Separation and divorce demand enormous amounts of time and emotional energy. This is not a solution for the weak.

Here are some additional questions for people with children.

First, what will a divorce cost them? Look at it from every angle: the pain of deprivation, financial comfort, changes in their home, loss of emotional security, less contact with their parents, grandparents, or other relatives.

And if you should stay together, what will that cost? How will it affect their attitudes to relationships? Will they ultimately see their parents as heroic or weak? Will it damage their teen and adult lives, or endanger their ability to sustain a marriage later, if they see you two hang in with a chronically unhappy relationship?

In fact, it is important to ask yourself, are they already showing negative results of the on-going stress of your relationship? Do you see any changes in how they are coping these days with those areas of their lives that might serve as warning signs of current stress and predictors of future trouble, such as school, chores, friendships, and the way they handle their emotions?

Tough questions, indeed, but inescapable when you're contemplating a tough decision like divorce.

A CLEAN DIVORCE

It is an overwhelming responsibility to decide to break up a marriage. But that is only the beginning. It is even harder to carry it out cleanly and kindly.

So here are some principles which will help you to manage it with as much grace as is possible under truly unhappy circumstances.

Let's begin with how you handle your lawyer. Remember, you hire the lawyer to give you advice (which you can choose to accept, or not) to prepare documents, and sometimes to take you through the courts. But you are in charge.

If possible hire a marital specialist, not someone who does "a bit of this and a bit of that." Specialists tend to know something about families and children, and that helps.

Unless you're hoping for a big showdown, steer clear of the so-called "gunslingers," who like to fight hard and fight dirty—all for the sake of their clients, of course. They can leave you and your ex with a lifetime of residual pain. And all the while, of course, the meter is running.

Above all, give your lawyer clear instructions. Never forget that he or she was trained in an adversarial system, which sees the other person as the guilty party. So if what you want is not revenge but a fair settlement, you will have to make sure your lawyer understands your point of view.

In all this, it is important to keep punishment out of the divorce. Of course you have been hurt by the other person, but now you are starting a new life. If you try to hurt back at this stage, you will only increase the amount of bitterness between you.

And if you have children, they will end up carrying that load throughout their lives. They are counting on you for a clean divorce.

HOW FAMILY MEDIATION HELPS

The face of divorce is changing for the better. A process that used to involve agonizing years of hostile manoeuvring is in the process of being humanized, speeded up, and gentled down. Decisions that used to be the prerogative of legal professionals are now made by the parties themselves. An important part of this picture is a new form of assistance for separating couples called family mediation.

In family mediation, separating couples are provided help in retrieving the power over their own lives from the lawyers, judges, and other court officials on which our society has been over-dependent in the past. The issues they can resolve using this process include custody of the children, the division of their assets, and arrangements for financial support.

One prominent jurist has said that no judge could hope to be as knowledgeable about these issues as the couple themselves. Increasingly, politicians, judges, lawyers, religious leaders, family therapists, and doctors have come to agree with him that, where possible, family disputes should not be settled by public officials. For the majority of people, mediation is the best and most logical resource during a separation.

How does mediation actually work? Typically, the couple visit a mediator several times over the period of a few weeks. The mediator helps them to clarify their opinions about the issues they have to settle and to listen to each other's point of view. The entire process is designed to help them avoid a win/lose situation, with the hostility that it inevitably creates.

The mediator makes no decisions for them, but brings to the process a well-schooled set of skills in helping couples reach agreement, a broad experience of how other couples have arranged their separations, and a profound understanding of the needs of children in these situations. Since most couples have no previous experience in these areas, they find an outsider's help is welcome, as they develop their own separation agreement.

In a large majority of mediation cases, the couple achieves a consensus on the issues they face, thus avoiding litigation, and they take away with them an agreement tailor-made to fit their unique circumstances.

Mediators may be lawyers, social workers, or therapists. They combine empathy for the adults with an understanding of the psychological effect of divorce on children.

Their basic guidelines for family mediation consist of two questions: What is fair? And if this marriage has to break up, what arrangements will be the very best for the children?

PRINCIPLES THAT MAKE MEDIATION WORK

Here are some of the principles which govern family mediation.

The participants must instruct their lawyers to hold off on pursuing legal solutions and to co-operate with the mediation in every possible way, so that they don't have to contend with legal manoeuvres, subpoenas, wrangling between lawyers, or court battles increasing the anger and mistrust between them. They want this difficult time to leave as few scars as possible.

To be effective, mediation requires honesty and trust. So the couple agree to reveal absolutely everything which might have a bearing on the process: money, property, even other relationships.

An essential aspect of mediation is compromise, but it is compromise of a very special sort, in that neither person is pressured to agree to a decision without considering all the factors.

Compromise is sometimes viewed as an "I give in; you win," situation. But because the stakes are so high here, often with children involved, both parties will end up making concessions in mediation. They should not be forced into compromises just to satisfy the mediator or their ex-spouse.

Understandably, people often feel a lot of hurt or anger at this time, but good mediators can help them channel those emotions so that they don't stand in the way of their task, which is to make decisions about the future, and most often, about their children.

In all this, the crucial principle is that the children's needs and rights deserve primary consideration. No matter how angry, hurt, or vulnerable the parents may feel, their decisions must have the children's best interests at heart.

PROS AND CONS OF MEDIATION

Here are some of the advantages of family mediation.

First of all, our legal system tends to be adversarial in nature. But mediation, instead of pitting an estranged wife and husband against each other, actually helps them co-operate in making crucial decisions about their children, their money, and their property.

And because they do that together, they have a personal commitment to their decisions, which tends to make them last better than arrangements ordered by the courts. Mediated settlements also leave less unresolved anger, and almost always cost less money than litigation.

Governments are beginning to recognize that family mediation can also reduce the logjams in our divorce courts.

There can also be disadvantages to mediation.

On rare occasions, a spouse may use the period of mediation to conceal financial assets. Or if the children live with only one parent during mediation, a legal status quo may result, which, if the case ultimately goes to court, could result in the other parent being awarded less time with them. Finally, some feminists have argued that mediation works against women married to violent men and those women who have been conditioned not to ask for what they really need.

Those arguments certainly point to the need for well-trained mediators, who are keenly aware of the potential dangers. But the consensus is clear: the advantages outnumber the disadvantages. Family mediation is here to stay, and will become increasingly popular.

PUTTING YOUR LIFE BACK TOGETHER

Often the end of a marriage seems to bring life to a crashing halt. Failure, hurt, grief: they are all too present. But is there life after divorce?

Here are some of the ways you can put your life back together, after your marriage breaks up.

One of the first things to take care of is your self-esteem. If you were to take to heart all the anger, all the criticisms that were thrown around as your marriage was ripping apart, you could end up thinking yourself an inadequate excuse for a human being and a totally substandard lover.

So one of your major tasks for the next stage of your life is to rebuild your feelings about yourself. It will help this process if you learn to be aware of the vibrations that others send out, and only allow those people close to you who are prepared to treat you like the precious human being you really are.

Furthermore, you are going to have some grieving to do for the loss of your hopes and dreams. During periods of grief, people are not light-hearted and easy-going; they have a lot to work through emotionally.

Yet sometimes they are tempted to hide their tears and pretend that nothing happened, usually "for the sake of others." At such times, it is not at all wise to play frantically at being happy, or to pretend to be a social butterfly, in an attempt to convince yourself or others that everything is okay.

Leave your stiff upper lip in the fridge; let yourself be what you are, an ordinary, vulnerable, human being.

Sooner or later, you will start to feel happier, meet new people, and even think about dating. If you were married for many years, that idea may seem strange and slightly frightening. Just take it step by step. Begin by double-dating with a friend you trust, and soon you will get the hang of it. Remember, dating doesn't require you to be super-cool and clever; your best asset is your natural self.

Yes, there is life after divorce. Give yourself time, and you will discover some of its special joys.

CHAPTER TEN

Society's Influence on Relationships

A middle-aged man entered my office recently, looking white and shaken. "I just found out that my best friends are breaking up," he said. "And last week, my brother and his wife split up. Explain it to me. What is happening to us?" No words could erase his pain, but hearing an explanation offered some comfort and helped him support those he loves.

What is happening to this man's friends and family, and to millions of others, is that our society is imposing rapid and radical changes on intimate relationships, transformations that may ultimately affect every family on this continent.

With friendships cracking at the seams, divorce statistics spiralling, and many surviving marriages desperately unhappy, it is important to examine some of the underlying social forces that encourage marital breakdown, so that concerned people can begin to counter them.

A CHANGING SOCIETY AFFECTS RELATIONSHIPS

The forces which buffet our relationships today are myriad. They include the reality of hard economic times which interlace confusingly with periods of affluence; disruptive long-distance job transfers; an ease of mobility and a privacy unprecedented in the history of civilization, which provides opportunities for styles of relationships so varied that they shake the primacy of marriage; the public acceptance of divorce and remarriage (not to mention re-divorce and re-remarriage); sparkling media images of the good life which seduce us into dissatisfaction; an electronics revolution which provides us with the tools to bring people and information together miraculously, but cannot warm our hearts.

As you come to understand these forces, you will be better prepared to comprehend what your children are dealing with, keep the lines of communication open with your own lovers, spouses, and families, make and maintain better friendships, and develop work relationships which will satisfy and nourish you.

All of this is more crucial than ever before. While our human relationships suffer massive shocks because of changes in our society, sometimes bend under the stress, and frequently end up changing radically, they remain the major sources of our happiness and the welcome supports for much of our lives. Where do we turn, when faced with anxiety, joy, sorrow, economic uncertainty, or the challenge imposed by a successful career? We turn to friends and to family.

But today, when we talk about family, we mean something different than before. The "nuclear family" no longer means a nucleus consisting of Mom, Dad, and their 2.3 children. Today it could equally refer to the family living under the threat of a thermonuclear holocaust. The old "Leave It To Beaver"/ "Father Knows Best" style of family, with its simple structure, has now been supplanted by combinations and permutations that Ozzie and Harriet would never recognize.

If the most obvious victim of societal change is marriage itself, some people wonder whether it constitutes the problem. Is marriage, as a formal, legally recognized union, outdated? Is it a fad that has passed its vogue?

The answer is, probably not. The difficulty seems to lie not with marriage but with the effects of a hostile environment on something even more basic: our fragile love relationships. Significantly, even where couples are living together unmarried (as more and more people, from teenagers to senior citizens, are doing) their relationships are not spared this instability.

Legally married or not, if a relationship doesn't make it, there are still too many people around who ignore the societal influences and take a simplistic view of tragedy. They say things like, "That couple never really tried hard enough," or "They shouldn't have argued so much, or had that affair, or tried to renovate their house."

These are people who get their kicks out of passing judgment on others. Their appraisals may at times be partially accurate, but they constitute cheap, easy criticism which offers no solutions. Because they lack empathy, they have nothing to offer people in pain, other than the dead weight of guilt.

If we as a society want the durability of our relationships to improve, we must struggle to understand the changes around us, which currently make it so difficult for even the most dedicated family people to maintain their long-term relationships.

That quality of understanding is both the gateway to empathy, and the best defense of our fragile loves against the devastating power of our society.

TRADITIONAL MARRIAGE SUPPORTS ERODE

Everyone is noticing how difficult it is today to keep love relationships as fresh and as joyful as they wish they could be. "Why?" people ask. "Why do couples keep falling apart?"

One reason is that, whether these couples are formally married, or living together, traditional support systems are increasingly unhelpful.

In every age, and on every continent, societies have depended on five basic forces to support marriage. And today, all five are being eroded by the shifts in our civilization.

Here they are:

First. Economic need, which means basically that two can live cheaper than one.

Today, people have more income, or, if they are needy, improved benefits from the state. They may not have an easy life as singles or single parents, but they seldom have to stay married in order to survive.

Second. The need for help, in raising children, raising crops, or running a business.

With the concentration of people in cities and suburban areas, there are more services accessible to substitute for the traditional spouse's role. With more money available to many, paid help is not so hard to find. In some cases, equipment like answering machines and intercoms are reducing the need for couples to be in two places at once.

Third. The need for companionship, for someone else just to be there.

With travel and communication easier than ever before, it is easier to meet people and fulfil that desire for intimacy. There are also enough distractions in our society that some people remain literally unaware of their needs for companionship.

Fourth. The need for someone to have sexual relations with.

The liberalization of moral standards has allowed many people to fulfil their sexual needs outside of marriage. Sexual release can come to be seen as a right, not a privilege.

Fifth. Society's demand for fidelity and stability, often expressed by fairly rigid rules about conduct, many of which were expressed through religion.

Church, synagogue, mosque and temple have suffered a massive decline in influence as people become more selective and independent about what they believe. The dwindling of their moral clout reflects a more general shift; many people find it difficult to believe in marriage-no-matter-what in a world where everything else is changing, where nothing is absolute.

So, as the twentieth century draws to a close, every one of those five traditional forces has lost some of its power to help cement relationships together. As a result, people no longer depend as they once did on the conventional role of the spouse.

THE QUEST FOR ROMANCE

While marriage and other long-term love relationships have had many of their traditional supports eroded in recent years, they have also been buffeted by a brand new set of pressures without precedent in Western history.

One of them I call the "Great Expectations Syndrome." To put it simply, we demand more from our love relationships than we ever have before. We especially desire passion and romance, and that desire is inflamed by the books, magazines, movies, advertising and television shows we see.

Beginning with the novels of D.H. Lawrence and early films such as *Gone with the Wind,* the quest for romance has become an increasingly powerful influence in the twentieth century. But the truth is that human beings have rarely found that real love is like our romantic ideals.

In fact, historically, romantic love has always been seen as a beautiful candle that first burns brightly—and then burns out. Only in relatively recent times have people seriously expected romance either to last or to sustain a marriage.

It is when the candle of romance burns out in a marriage, as it often does, that people start looking around for an affair, for someone new to rekindle that fire. What begins then, as a spark between two new lovers, erupts into "a flame with such a burning desire, that only your kiss can put out the fire."

Well, that's what the song claims, but we all know that the kiss is not going to extinguish anything, except maybe the original marriage.

Much of my work with couples is helping them maintain the romance in their marriages. I believe in passion. But in some cases, impossibly great expectations of romance combine with other pressures to wreck today's fragile relationships.

SELF-RESPECT AND SELF-ESTEEM

People suffering from "Great Expectations Syndrome" want more from their lovers than most people can deliver, and the consequences for their families are in some cases tragic. Yet despite the pain, there is also something very healthy—and in any case, unavoidable—about rising expectations.

More than ever before, people are looking around to decide what they want from their relationships, and then "going for it." Urged on first by the women's movement, and then by the men's, they are refusing to tolerate negative relationships: those which hold them back from their full emotional and sexual potential; those in which they are physically or emotionally abused, or where their children are in danger; and those from which care and respect are lacking.

And as self-respect grows into self-esteem, many would prefer to take their chances as single people, or even as single parents, than to stay in marriages that they feel are destroying them.

They are leaving relationships that, in some cases, are a living hell, in others, just deadly boring. As one frustrated but still-married woman said recently, "All I'm looking for is someone I can talk with about ideas."

Is this new attitude narcissism? Or is it self-respect? You will have to decide. But of this you can be sure, in the history of the human race, there has never been anything like it. While most evident in Europe and North America, it is spreading rapidly to the Third World.

It is the inevitable, though unexpected, by-product of the spread of ideas, a natural consequence of the explosion of information about relationships and of the mass marketing of desire.

MEDIA: CHANGING OUR MINDS ABOUT MARRIAGE

Sometimes people think that the "information explosion" is only a clever buzz-word thought up by public relations people. But this "explosion" is very real and it poses a down-to-earth threat to family life.

When men first walked on the moon, a friend of mine watched the event on television in a tiny mud-walled hut belonging to peasants in an out-of-the-way village in rural Mexico.

That has always been a powerful metaphor to me for the information explosion. Before broadcasting, only those few who could read had access to information about what was happening beyond the boundaries of their own experience.

Today, with radio and television, satellites and video, even those millions who are still illiterate can enjoy the dramas, the music, the commercial dreams, and the news broadcasts which subtly influence our social fabric.

In practical terms this also means that, if a Hollywood producer gets the urge to add another episode of marriage break-down, adultery, or incest to his soap opera, many millions of people, viewers all around the globe, may find their values affected by it.

On a scale unknown before, we know what happens in other people's relationships and imaginations. That, in itself, is earth-shaking. Inevitably, it means that people will see that there are other options for their lives than those prescribed by their village, religion, or family.

Although there is a natural backlash against the resulting changes in relationships, as seen for instance in the upsurge of Christian and Islamic fundamentalism, it is unlikely to do more than delay the inescapable.

In this new global village, there is lots of village gossip on the air. Believing in too much of it could turn us all into village idiots. But the information explosion is unstoppable, and with it will go one of the major supports for long-term stable relationships.

AFFLUENCE AND MARRIAGE

One factor making it increasingly difficult to keep our love relationships in good health is that our contemporary affluence interferes with the way we feel about each other.

Solemn people used to intone that, "Money can't buy happiness." Then some joker would chime in, "But at least it makes misery a lot more comfortable." Once I would have agreed with the joker, but my clinical work reminds me that affluence can actually make for more misery, contributing to the erosion of our most important relationships.

There is, of course, nothing new about marriage breakdown or divorce. What is new is that almost everyone has more money and owns more things.

Perhaps you have noticed the new term: "adult toys." What it means is that people can afford more expensive play things. Whether the "toys" are computers, motorcycles, Caribbean cruises, fancy sweaters, or supermarket romances, it is a sign that we are giving more attention than ever before to material possessions that can distract us from the human beings we love.

Our prosperity is bound to affect our values, because, in times of affluence, people easily forget that the two most priceless possessions anyone can own are self-esteem and a great love.

When you can buy most anything you want, it is harder to be patient with human relationships, where money can't solve the problems or satisfy the yearning.

Today, when people have money for gas, and more money for jet plane tickets, it is easier to escape from those you love, for extended periods of time. Sometimes, to twist another proverb, absence makes the heart grow colder.

In the midst of all this, there is one commodity that is a lot cheaper these days. Divorce.

So, despite our growing affluence, these are certainly hard times for marriage.

TIME AND MARRIAGE

Time is so short.

If only the clock had a couple of extra numbers on it. Or if we didn't spend a third of our lives asleep. If only our careers didn't take so many hours. Why then we would have enough time for the people we love the most.

Or would we?

You would not expect an experienced therapist to be shocked by very much in human behaviour, but I am frequently rocked by the number of couples who say they don't have time to spend with each other. These couples rarely sit silently together or touch gently, or talk about their feelings, dream dreams, or make love.

Instead they stay up so late watching television that they have to go to bed early the next night. They clean their homes till they're spotless or stay late at the office, they go to a bar after work with their friends or work out alone at the gym, they attend meetings at the church or other worthy causes, they putter aimlessly about the house, or bury themselves in books, computers, and briefcases.

As the routine "housekeeping" of their lives takes over, their love becomes a pale, gaunt shadow of what it was once, in the days when wild horses couldn't keep them from whispering in each other's ears and looking endlessly into each other's eyes.

Marriages get sick when people find time and energy for everything else but love. In fact, one vital ingredient that couples need, is time to be successful.

THE ASCENT OF AMBITION

In this new society of ours, the career has turned out to be a major threat to marriage.

Throughout much of human history, couples held together if they could raise enough food to eat, keep relatively healthy, and protect their children from a dangerous world. The greatest ambition of most people was to survive.

But the perspective of today's affluent societies is very different. Most people now live above the subsistence level, and their expectations of what they need in order to be happy have escalated.

Some one-track minds like to hint that the increasing incidence of marital problems is the fault of the feminist movement. If women would just put their families first, they say, everything would be "fine," which really means "the way it used to be." But the truth is that both men and women are becoming increasingly ambitious, and the trend is unlikely to abate.

Being better educated, they demand more from their work: self-fulfillment, personal satisfaction, and a sense of accomplishment. It is hard to argue with a person wanting those rewards. But the down side is that, when the career is hot, marriage is sometimes relegated to the back burner, out of sight, out of mind.

As well, career people are often frightened by the rugged demands, and the relentless competition of the marketplace. They fear they'll be out-paced by their fellow workers, out-placed by their employers, and finally replaced. So, hoping to preserve their standing, they too often give their hearts and souls to the corporation—not to mention their evenings and weekends.

And there goes the marriage. Ambition, abetted by anxiety, is unlikely to decline. Wise couples will balance its strident demands with the quieter solaces of affection.

HOW THE FAMILY PRESSURES THE COUPLE

Joining together in couples has developed among human beings for two important and obvious reasons. One is to provide pleasure and support to the adults. And the other is to provide a stable, nurturing nest for children to grow up in. Otherwise, we could mate like fish, then swim away.

The nesting plan is a good theory, but today's harsh reality is that the needs of the children can actually weaken the nest, and potentially destroy the couple they depend on.

If you have ever felt yourself so occupied with the children that you had neither the time nor the energy to communicate with your wife or husband, then you know what I'm talking about. Naturally, we all want the best for our children, but that can create tremendous demands on us.

To take just one common example, some suburban parents operate a virtually endless bus service for their young children. "Next stop swimming lessons!" Or karate. Or art club. Or special classes. Or the homes of their children's pals. The list of stops is endless, like the rest of their parental duties.

So when do adults find time to refresh their love and romance? Squeezed in between the late-night news and falling asleep exhausted.

Or more often, squeezed right out. In these situations, it is no surprise when their emotional energy gets diverted from nurturing their relationship toward just keeping up with kids.

And no surprise that marriages can get sick just when the family needs them most.

MARITAL GLUE

These pages are intended to encourage those who are feeling the stress of keeping relationships healthy, to remind you that you are not alone and that the difficulties you face are not all your fault.

Inexorable forces are moulding your life.

As a result of improvements in medicine and the increase in life expectancy, when you make promises to love each other "till death do us part," you are committing yourself to keep your marriage healthy for approximately twice as long as the typical marriage lasted at the turn of the century. In itself, that is no mean feat.

And although you will then be blown about by the radical changes and relentless pressures of contemporary society, you have to cope with them using emotional equipment that has developed little since the days when humans lived in caves. The miracle of our emotions lies in their adaptability and sophistication, but they still remain primitive tools to cope with a super-complex life, and the stress often shows.

Further, in this age, there is less glue holding families together. As the global village expands and our guiding rules and religions weaken, our relationships are all more likely to suffer stress fractures. At the same time our children's world is becoming more dark and dangerous, so their legitimate demands for attention are on the increase.

Given all this, no wonder it is difficult to keep marriages healthy.

And no wonder that alert couples are coming to realize that you cannot simply allow important relationships to drift. To keep your marriage healthy means staying alert, taking responsibility for yourself, and recognizing that, as a couple you need, in fact deserve, the benefits of every resource your intelligence and our society offer.

This must be the toughest time in history for marriages. May yours more than survive. May it be healthy and strong.

CHAPTER ELEVEN

You're the Therapist

The theme throughout this book is that you can be your own therapist. Therapy is quite simply the maintenance of mental and emotional health and the healing of wounds. As you naturally and spontaneously nurture your relationships and tend the garden of your emotions, you are inevitably engaged in the process of therapy. This is not at all the exclusive property of professionals.

At the same time, the therapy profession is available to help, if you should want a skillful partner in the task. Under the right conditions, working with a good psychotherapist can speed the work and, most important, provide a superb opportunity for you to hone your skills as a self-therapist.

SELF-THERAPY AND PROFESSIONAL THERAPY

Everyone needs a highly refined set of skills if they want to do more than just survive in this difficult world, and as you become your own therapist, you are learning those skills. People who are their own therapists know how their emotions affect them, understand what is happening with their relationships and how to deal with them, and can communicate in a deep and satisfying way with their loved ones.

The practice of therapy is no more restricted to professional therapists than the preservation of your physical health is the responsibility of doctors alone. Good physical health begins and ends with you; you maintain it with such ordinary routines as practicing good hygiene, getting enough sleep, drinking clean water, and keeping dirt out of your cuts. You generally go to see a doctor only if you want help in understanding some aspect of your health or if you are ill.

Similarly, ordinary people, in ordinary ways, have always been therapists to their own lives and relationships. They do not have to rely on therapists to cope with their day-to-day lives.

This approach contradicts the popular assumption that we ought to hand over the most crucial jobs in our society to the "experts." It is amazing that this idea prevails, when we have seen so many scandals in political life result from such an attitude. Over and over again, as a society, we have discovered that certain so-called experts turn out to be fanatical, self-centred, semi-competent, half-blind, or corrupt. By thoughtlessly entrusting them with crucial decisions, we have, in a way, entrapped them, provided them with opportunities for mischief that they should never have been offered.

Worse still, we have cheated ourselves of opportunities to become all that we reasonably can.

Now, it is true that in a complex world we cannot do everything ourselves. For some, because the idea of learning auto mechanics lies at the very bottom of their entertainment list, it seems worthwhile to take their cars to service stations instead. Others sensibly patronize professional lawyers, shoe repairers, and builders. The awkwardness of performing brain surgery on oneself while anaesthetized will lead others still to hire professional brain surgeons when needed. These decisions all make sense.

But in this world where we leave so much up to the experts, it is a tempting fallacy to believe that the real therapists are the professionals. In fact, nothing could be less true. As intelligent human beings, we are called by nature to be the primary therapists for our lives.

As you spend even 90 seconds each day consciously choosing to be your own primary therapist, reading and pondering the ideas in this book, you will find that you are becoming a more effective healer both for yourself and for your relationships with those you love. Maintaining your emotional health will become more like second nature, a form of hygiene as regular as brushing your own teeth. You wouldn't dream of visiting your dentist each time your teeth needed a scrub.

But once the principle is well established that you are your own primary therapist, it may be useful to look at the ways in which an outsider, a professionally trained therapist, might be of legitimate help to you. As with physical medicine, there may be points in your life when the therapy profession can provide something special in the way of support and help. That possibility is what this section is about.

The three situations which most commonly propel people into professional therapy are these: coping with serious emotional problems, undertaking an intensive time of self-learning, and treating a troubled relationship.

COPING WITH SERIOUS EMOTIONAL PROBLEMS

If you are in urgent emotional trouble, for instance if you are suffering from serious mood swings, acute depression, severe anxiety, or violent or suicidal thoughts, you certainly ought to be seeing a therapist. Therapy is no more optional for you than a doctor is an option for someone suffering a heart attack.

The self-therapy theme of this book is not intended to pressure you to try to make it on your own. While *The 90-Second Therapist* can help you begin to cope with deep personal crises, it cannot replace the reassuring presence of a competent professional therapist. The safest, most comforting, and most effective way to be your own therapist in these circumstances is to learn the skills of self-therapy through a professional relationship.

Please, do not let pride complacency, or fear keep you from getting the best help. Do not take risks with your life, your happiness, or your loved ones.

AN INTENSIVE TIME OF SELF-LEARNING

There may be times in your life when you are motivated to learn more about the complicated human being you are by tapping the wisdom of an experienced therapist, using him or her as a spiritual teacher or mentor. Often the desire to do this is stimulated by a crisis: a failure, the loss of love, a disappointment, a rejection.

A therapist will be alert to help you see the motifs in your life history which may limit your scope as a person. With the clarity an outsider can bring to the task, your therapist can help you discover how you yourself may have set up some of the crises that hurt you and undermine your self-confidence. Understanding these themes in your life can provide you with many more options for the future.

Attitude is everything here. Working with a therapist is not like taking your car to a mechanic, who may perform the work competently but leave you just as blissfully ignorant of how a vehicle functions. Here you use the therapist's skills not as a substitute for your own initiative, but as a deliberate extension of your care for yourself. You learn the tricks of the trade from someone who knows them well.

This does not mean putting yourself passively "into the hands of the professionals," but making a crucial spiritual decision to take matters into your own hands, to become your own "mechanic" with the aid of this highly skilled assistant.

TREATING A TROUBLED RELATIONSHIP

If a relationship is stuck in destructive patterns or is in danger of falling apart, professional therapy may be useful to you.

Often it is hard to recognize by yourself the patterns that damage your friendships or family ties. This is where a skilled third party, someone who is objective but warm, caring but not dependent on you, can cast new light on old problems, and help you make effective plans for change.

In addition, because you are developing a lively and intimate relationship with the therapist, this is the perfect environment in which you can clarify some of the patterns with which you relate to your loved ones. It also gives you a safe, controlled opportunity to practise new ways of communicating with someone who is important to you.

This "live" quality brings a challenging reality test—"Am I really changing?"—into the midst of your learning process.

HOW TO FIND A GOOD THERAPIST

There is a cynical old story about the therapist who listens to his client for a few minutes and then replies, "So, you think you've got problems...." He then proceeds to talk his client's ear off about his own unhappy marriage.

In fact, therapy horror stories abound: about therapists who get into power struggles with their clients, who take them to bed, who encourage a prolonged dependent relationship, who fail to protect the family system that their clients are part of, or who impose their own value systems.

There are tales about professionals who routinely encourage the use of drugs when the better choice would be psychotherapy, and about people who flaunt the relevant degrees but possess no talent. Some talk a good line, but cannot practice what they preach.

People like this are, thankfully, a tiny minority, but if you have decided to further the process of becoming your own therapist by working with a professional, you will certainly want to avoid them.

So how do you locate a therapist who fits the essential specifications: well-trained, ethical, sensible, and good at the job?

With some difficulty.

Even though the majority of therapists are both ethical and responsible, in many jurisdictions anyone who fancies himself or herself to be a therapist can hang out a shingle, without submitting to any set of standards or regulations. In other words, you will find scores of therapists listed in the Yellow Pages or the personal columns, but there is no guarantee that they are competent.

One way around this information gap is to consult professionals whose opinion you trust and who routinely refer people for therapy, like your doctor, lawyer, or minister. Ask a few key questions: "Did you get any feedback from other people you sent to this therapist?" "What do they say?" "Do you think this person would work well with my kind of personality?" And the best question of all, "Would you send a close friend or near relative to this therapist?"

If you can't get a good referral this way, professional associations of doctors, psychologists, and psychotherapists list those who are qualified according to their particular standards and are subject to their code of ethics. For instance, the local office of the American Association For Marriage And Family Therapy can inform you of qualified couple and family counsellors in your area.

The very best source of information is often a trusted friend or relative who has actually worked with a particular therapist. Because this person knows the therapist from direct experience, he or she will have a better idea of how the two of you might work out together. He or she can also provide you with information which a professional association cannot, information about how the therapist actually functions in the office.

Finally though, you will have to make your own assessment. Generally that involves making and paying for a first appointment. Here are some questions you should ask:

"What are your qualifications and education?" "How much supervision of your work have you had?" "Do you routinely consult with colleagues about your on-going cases?" (These questions will help you weed out the Lone Ranger types who tend to see things from their own very narrow perspective.)

"How would you describe your style and philosophy?" "Do you have any personal biases about divorce (or child custody, feminism, affairs, homosexuality, or whatever other issues you bring with you into therapy)?"

"How will we actually spend these hours?" (If the therapist proposes sitting behind a desk or out of your sight, check him or her out further. This may be a person who isn't secure and doesn't make good contact.) "How much do you charge; when and how do I pay you; what happens if I miss an appointment?"

Having asked your questions and explained your issues, you must then rely on your own perceptions and reactions.

A good therapist makes good eye contact, lets you know that he or she really understands you. No matter how much you may think yourself a failure, your therapist appreciates you as a person and believes in your potential.

The right therapist for you is someone you feel comfortable with. He or she may challenge you and ask awkward, even embarrassing, questions at times, but down deep you must know that the therapist is on your side, one hundred per cent.

That's a gut feeling, hard to explain in words, but without heart-level trust, nothing very valuable ever happens in therapy.

Finally, good therapists have almost always been in therapy themselves, have struggled like you to grow and change, and, because of that, understand something of what it is like for you to be in therapy.

A FAMILY APPROACH TO THERAPY

Jody and Donna were worried about their six-year-old daughter Jenny. She constantly misbehaved, sometimes with a defiant grin on her face, and at times she hurt other children.

When they took her to the hospital for assessment, drugs were prescribed which calmed her down. An appointment was also made for Jenny to enter individual psychotherapy.

But Jody and Donna knew in their hearts that a prescription was not the answer. Jenny's problems were not caused by a chemical imbalance in her body.

They also had a hunch that individual psychotherapy was the wrong tool to treat her problems.

So they found themselves a family therapist and over a period of time began to make changes that helped Jenny's health improve.

As they thought about their own home, they saw how their constant involvement in their own fights left their daughter without much attention.

Perverse as it was, her misbehaviour had worked. It gave her exactly the thing that a little child needs, which is attention.

On the other hand, because of their anger at each other, Jody and Donna usually contradicted one another's efforts at discipline. This left their six-year-old deeply confused about how to behave, making "her" problem far worse.

Her violent streak had an unexpected advantage which might have prolonged her unhappiness in conventional treatment. This "benefit" was that their worry about Jenny united her parents, as nothing else could do.

So in a strange but common way, her problems had real advantages for the family as a whole. Which is why they persisted.

Jenny's violent episodes happened, in other words, not because she was a bad kid, but because her parents were at war. And as the focus shifted away from the child to the parents, and as they began the hard work of rebuilding their trust and love, Jenny gradually got better.

Despite a whole century of progress in the development of psychotherapy, only in the past few decades has there existed a sufficiently sophisticated form of therapy to treat family illnesses, as opposed to trying to treat, or medicate, the Jennys of this world.

Psychotherapy itself is a recent development in the annals of human thinking. Throughout the centuries, ancient shamans, medicine women and men, witches, priests, and doctors all practiced therapy, but in a hit-and-miss manner, and only as a sideline to their major work. Until the turn of the century, the world still awaited a comprehensive, subtle, and practical approach which would help human beings deal with their mental and emotional hurts.

When psychotherapy began to emerge, it was an individualistic practice shaped by the limited experience of the medical doctors who developed it. Their conception was pretty artificial: one patient, one diagnosis, like a planet spinning alone in space, or an island isolated in the midst of an ocean.

The early therapists, beginning with Freud, were too busy developing their new science to see the patient as part of a system.

So while they recognized from the beginning that families often make individuals ill, they had no idea what to do with those families. They might blame the parents of their patients for their neuroses, but they usually had no plan for treating the family.

The famous poet John Donne expressed the essential notion which would come to govern family therapy when he wrote in 1624, "No man is an island, entire of itself." Every one of us, he said, "is a piece of the continent." And so, if a clod of earth is washed away by the sea, each of us is diminished.

As family therapy began to develop over the past few decades, its practitioners saw people not as solitary individuals, but as part of that "continent" or system that includes their family, friends, and the people at school or work.

Family therapists paid attention to how the members of the "continent" affect each other. And they helped them improve once-troubled relationships so that they become a source of strength.

Because family therapy sees people as part of a complex of relationships, such issues as cause and effect, blame, fault, responsibility, and reward are viewed in a broader perspective.

Whether or not you ever feel the need for formal marriage and family therapy, you will find that its way of looking at relationships provides the essential perspective for anyone who wants to be a 90-Second Therapist.

THE ADVENTURE OF THERAPY

Have you ever wondered what it would be like to be in psychotherapy? Because it is such a private experience, taking place behind closed doors, only those who have actually experienced it can describe it faithfully.

Therapy is, first of all, a meeting of equals, a relationship of mutual respect. My clients are ordinary and wonderful, troubled and neurotic, just like you and I are. So there is just no room for the therapist to feel distant and superior.

In fact, the best therapist is more like a friend, a professional friend to be sure, to the client. That is very important to people who feel isolated and lonely. In the therapist's office they discover community and often a higher level of acceptance than they accord themselves.

There are limitations to a professional friendship, of course; the fee, the boundaries of time and touch, the inevitable termination. But even those have their advantages. These limits allow for a certain distance, a caring objectivity. Because therapists do not need their clients to fulfil their own desires, they can encourage them to travel their own chosen roads without any strings attached.

Actually, that is not a bad metaphor. You could do worse than describe therapy as an adventure, a trip through the uncharted territory of a human heart and its relationships. Like any voyage, it requires expenditure, courage, and openness of spirit. It is an exploration not suitable for the faint-hearted nor for those who are content to let their lives drift on without direction or hope. In fact, therapy is effective only for people who are profoundly committed to finding a more abundant life.

In this exploration, there are always surprises along the way, of course, sometimes the pain of half-forgotten memories revived, sometimes a sense of emotional danger. But people in therapy find they can handle the risks, because they are secure in the support of their therapist, and because the goal of their therapy is to discover hidden treasure, treasure that is waiting to be found within their own personalities.

Those who are engaged in therapy, both therapist and client, value the adventurous child in every one of us, appreciate the adult wisdom we have each collected on our path through life, and understand that even our most unlikely personal qualities may turn out to be the finest gold.

Toronto Centre for the Family

The Toronto Centre For The Family is a private agency which provides therapy for individuals, couples, and families, in a warm, comfortable atmosphere. Co-directors are Esther Kohn-Bentley M.Ed. and Timothy Bentley M.Div. Believing that each human being is precious, they are committed to create an atmosphere of respect for their clients, confidence in their innate strengths, and hope for the future.

THE VISITORS INTENSIVE PROGRAM (VIP)

The Visitors Intensive Program is for people who are highly motivated to make changes in their lives, but reside too far away to schedule weekly therapy visits at the Toronto Centre For The Family. VIP provides a special weeklong opportunity for intensive therapy, consisting of five two-hour sessions beginning on a Monday and ending that Friday, with plenty of free time left over to enjoy the sights and culture of Toronto. Write for details.

YOU AND ME AUDIOTAPES

The Toronto Centre For The Family's You and Me audiotapes feature husband and wife team Timothy Bentley and Esther Kohn-Bentley talking personally to couples who want to increase their intimacy, in the privacy of their homes. In the first tape, "You and Me—Good Together," the Bentleys help their listeners reflect on and celebrate their past life together. In "You and Me—Better Still," they lead couples through a number of helpful exercises designed to lower their barriers and re-experience the warmth they have shared. Along the way, listeners meet such familiar and amusing marital characters as Millie the Mindreader and Justin the Judge.

To order each set of two You and Me cassette tapes, send $15.95 plus $2.00 for postage and handling to the Toronto Centre For The Family. Ontario residents add $1.12 sales tax.

Toronto Centre For The Family
Post Office Box 664, Station "P",
Toronto, Ontario M5S 2Y4,
Canada   (416) 923-5021